ON DIALOGUE

ON DIALOGUE

An Essay in Free Thought

✌

Robert Grudin

A Richard Todd Book

HOUGHTON MIFFLIN COMPANY

Boston New York

1996

For information about permission to reproduce selections from
this book, write to Permissions, Houghton Mifflin Company,
215 Park Avenue South, New York, New York 10003.

For information about this and other Houghton Mifflin trade and reference
books and multimedia products, visit The Bookstore at
Houghton Mifflin on the World Wide Web at
http://www.hmco.com/trade/.

Library of Congress Cataloging-in-Publication Data

Grudin, Robert.
On dialogue : an essay in free thought / Robert Grudin.
p. cm.
Includes bibliographical references (p.) and index.
ISBN 0-395-77187-0
1. Conduct of life.   2. Dialogue.   I. Title.
BJ1595.G854 1996
110 — dc20   96-990   CIP

Book design by Anne Chalmers
Set in Adobe Garamond

Printed in the United States of America

QUM 10 9 8 7 6 5 4 3 2 1

To Charles and Doris Muscatine

Contents

ͻͼͻͼͻͼͻͼͻ

PART THREE

DIALOGUE AND FREEDOM
IN SCIENCE AND
PHILOSOPHY

Preface

⟲⟳⟲⟳⟲⟳

This is a book about various forms of dialogue. It deals with familiar dialogues — talks between lovers or peers or teachers and students — and unfamiliar ones: dialogues between science and nature, between author and text, between species and environment. Repeatedly, moreover, I have been drawn to consider dialogues *occurring within a single mind* — dialogues between perspectives and modalities within a single awareness. My premise is that dialogue on all of these levels is consciousness-raising and liberating, and hence that dialogue is an essential component of liberty.

This project took shape in Berkeley, California, during the academic year 1992–1993. I am grateful to the John Simon Guggenheim Foundation for a fellowship supporting this project and to the University of Oregon for the sabbatical leave that made it possible. Additional support was provided by the Fetzer Institute, the Humanities Center at the University of Oregon and the English Department of the University of California at Berkeley. I am grateful to Franz von Hammerstein-Equord and Gottfried Paasche for introducing me to the work of Martin Buber. My sincere thanks go to Charles Muscatine and John Beebe, for their detailed and thoughtful comments on the manuscript, and to my Houghton Mifflin editor Richard Todd, who, as a writer and teacher himself, has a special way of reading, and to Liz Duvall and Mindy Keskinen. Finally I wish to express my gratitude to my wife, Michaela Paasche Grudin, whose simultaneous project, *Chaucer and the Politics of Discourse* (University of South Carolina Press, 1996), has been a continuous source of inspiration.

ON DIALOGUE

I

❧❧❧

Introduction:
Dialogue and Freedom

DIALOGUE AND THE FREE MIND

"The world," remarked Abraham Lincoln, "has never had a good definition of the word liberty." He might have added that in one sense such a definition suggests a profound contradiction in terms. To define is to circumscribe, to limit. Is it reasonable to limit the one idea that embodies centuries of human discomfort with limitation?

Yet we *can* discuss liberty by means of its attributes and its endangerments. Imagine an aboriginal tribesman abducted from the bush and locked up in some urban facility, and he will give you a clearer picture of liberty than you will find in Jefferson or Rousseau. "Give me back my land," he will say. "Give me back my people; give me back my body; give me back my days." Liberty is a specific relationship between humanity and its natural/social environment: a relationship in which human needs can be gratified and human aspirations expressed to the fullest possible extent. To be free is to have the chance to be human. Take this from us and we cease to be ourselves.

But while liberty is a constant, the human needs and aspirations that address it are widely varied. The bushman's freedom may well exist in a society where authority is centralized and discourse is limited. American liberty, in contrast, is predicated on free thought and political equality. To a large extent these two key benefits are interdependent. We cannot think freely if basic advantages like education and expression are awarded to some of us and denied to others. We cannot live as equals without the vigilance and oversight of unimpeded inquiry. Our aspirations, our sense of our own humanity, demand this ambitious combination of guarantees.

But "free thought" and "equality" are relative terms. To think absolutely freely, one would have to be all-knowing, all-seeing — an image of God. Conversely, we could not be completely equal unless we were ageless hermaphroditic clones, without families and under stringent laws at that. Moreover, the mere practice of free thought generates individuation, autonomous action and hence inequality. We must, then, find our way between two extremes: the excessive individual liberty that would leave us a people of masters and serfs, and the excessive emphasis on equality that would sap us of ambition and character.

This challenging interplay of opposed principles complicates the idea of liberty and defies all simple and conventional definitions of its character. Liberty is not a guaranteed privilege; it is not a condition that citizens are born into. Liberty is more aptly construed as an art, or rather a network of arts: arts by which individuals and groups can gain awareness of their own condition, preserve it and improve it. The mere existence of liberal laws and strong guarantees of individual scope is not a sure sign that these arts will flourish. As events in eastern Europe and Asia have shown us recently, the replacement of oppressive regimes by democratic structures is only the beginning, the foundation of the practice of liberty. Freedom is like making music: having an instrument, time and fingers isn't quite enough. You must learn an ancient skill that requires commitment, instruction and practice. The performance that, to the audience watching and listening, seems almost magical is achieved in slow steps, over many years. Once gained, moreover, the arts of freedom must be kept fresh by thought and action, taught to the young, bequeathed down generations. Otherwise the eternal parasites of freedom, the posturing demagogue, the ravenous mass-marketer, will turn liberty into its own caricature, a barbarous fool driven by fear and greed.

From early on, forms of these arts, known as *artes liberales,* "the arts of free people" or "the arts that give freedom," developed in the Western tradition. Analysis and expression are included in the first sequence of these (*trivium* or "three ways"); the second sequence (*quadrivium,* "four ways") includes the other arts and the sciences. The operative pedagogical philosophy is that skill in these arts will enable people to make decisions and follow courses of action beneficial to themselves and society. In other words, people can *learn freedom.* Freedom is useless without a rational and emotional instrumentation that gives it substance.

These arts of freedom are necessarily arts of the mind, and by "mind" here I mean our reasoning apparatus in conjunction with our emotions, our language and our values. These arts are essential for the survival of political liberty not only because they fulfill and maintain the liberty of a given culture but because they alone enable us to discern the changing forms of liberty and constraint in history. Free institutions can grow lax or oppressive, free vocabularies can inflate or be corrupted, all while maintaining the public semblance of liberty. Only the free mind, inquiring, questioning, can grasp these changes and announce them and conceive projects of renewal.

But is any mind truly free? The instrumentation of mental freedom consists of the languages and idea systems we use to frame, evaluate or describe our actions. One can view these languages and systems as established pathways guiding the flow of mental energy. Yet by virtue of being established, these instruments necessarily limit freedom. Pathways, designed for swift access from point to point, ignore the untrodden areas between and beyond them. Systems of any sort tend to grow self-protective, unfriendly to the new. Vast systems that seem just and effective can turn out to be huge conspiracies of collective ignorance, or cynical artifices of power.

Overshadowing these restrictive systems, and to some extent supporting them, is the lure of security. Just as the citizen is drawn to the safe haven, the warm cottage, the regular income, the trusting relationship, the mind is drawn to the consistent argument, the plausible explanation, the documented position, the unified picture. The mind feels secure in an interpretive context that is rational and self-coherent, a context that holds no explicit self-contradictions. "Common sense" is such a context; determinism, idealism and pragmatism are others. Each of these systems purports to explain everything; each is, within its own perspective and vocabulary, irrefutable. But by the same token, each system can become mental tyranny that narrows vision and condemns the mind to mechanical responses. The natural human desire for certainty and security is thus the root of ideology and dogma. It is said that "the truth will set you free," but here, paradoxically, we have versions of truth that enslave.[1]

---

1. The pitfalls of a fixed and limited perspective were first explored systematically in ancient Greece (anecdotally, first by Parmenides and his student Socrates; in extant writing, first by Socrates' student Plato). The standard contemporary work on the subject is Thomas Kuhn's *The Structure of Scientific Revolutions*. What is especially helpful about Kuhn's work is his understanding that a given perspective or "paradigm," no matter how limited it may seem to us, was of great practical value in its own time. (Paul Feyerabend takes this view to an extreme when, in *Against Method*, Chapter 13, he argues for the rationality of the Inquisition.) The critique of culturally fixed perspectives is standard practice among "postmodern" writers such as Michel Foucault (see Chapter 6) and the New Historicists, though their historical methods generally are not as careful as Kuhn's.

Thus the mind cannot be liberated from constraint until it is freed from its own inner tyrannies. How can we speak of such a freed awareness? The most accurate and least confusing adjective would be "dialogic." We generally think of dialogue as a communicative process involving two or more people, but more recently the word "dialogic" has been extended to processes going on within a single mind. The premise for this usage is the existence of inner voices or viewpoints, which, while sharing the memory and consciousness of the same person, can maintain some independence from each other. Elementary examples of dialogic interaction would be, say, conscience versus desire, liberal versus conservative, the parent in us versus the child in us; but inner dialogues may have more than two participants, and disagreement among them is not a necessary factor.

We are all affected by these multiple voices, whose polyphonic interplay gives our thought its character. But only the dialogic mind is consciously open to them and can, without prejudging the conclusion, give an ear to their proceedings. A mind thus open is unconstrained by monolithic canons, playful, reflective and capable of limitless variety. Indeed, awareness of inner multiplicity becomes a special form of self-awareness. This self-seeing is itself a dialogic process in which the mind momentarily surrenders its pretension to coherence in an effort to understand and refine its responses.

Thus conceived, the dialogic mind is not only a guardian of liberty but metaphorically similar to a democratic state. It rejects the tyranny of a single system or dogma; it welcomes new ideas and guarantees them equality as it considers them; it provides an open forum for competing theories and systems; it refuses to censor "dangerous" ideas; it cherishes and protects its capacity to learn and to grow; it guards as something precious its own access to joy and laughter.

At the heart of dialogic thought are two opposed but complementary principles which strangely mirror the equality and free-dom of the American republic. These principles can be called amplitude and independence. "Amplitude" connotes the desire to see a given topic *from every possible perspective;* it also connotes curiosity about and compassion for the minds of other people and other ages. "Independence" suggests the alienation felt by a mind that cannot rest long in any safe haven, together with the humor, delight and exhilaration of an autonomous awareness. The inter-action of amplitude and independence gives rise to a kind of chivalry of thought: to a spirit schooled equally in gentility and aggressiveness.

How is dialogic thinking learned? This book discusses a number of teaching approaches that are already in place, as well as a num-ber of self-teaching strategies.

DIALOGUE AND THE FREE SOCIETY

I lie in bed with a bad case of flu. My room is pleasant, and after a while the pain and fever give way to bronchitis, which calls for a few more days of rest. My wife, who takes care of me, my children, who visit my room, are now more sympathetic, less dependent on me than when I was well; my office has been informed, and my colleagues have promised to leave me alone until I rejoin them. As I lie in bed, peaceful solitary days slip by. I am amazed by the way my house, my business, which seemed so contingent on my ef-forts, now run happily without me. I read the newspaper, but from my isolated place in space/time, even local events seem to be happening in another world. Gradually I begin to feel vacuous, unnecessary. Am I really Robert Grudin? Certainly not Grudin the supporting father, not Grudin the indispensable colleague. Sud-denly I feel imprisoned; I yearn to be up and out — to reassert an identity that has begun to erode. *I am not free without my obligations.*

This paradox and others like it operate throughout the interface between individual and society. Individual identity is rooted in a communal substratum and asserted in culturally derived language and signs; individual autonomy is conducted according to socially generated values; even defiance and revolution are grounded in historical precedent. We are individuals not in spite of culture but because of culture, and the dialogue between self and society proceeds even in times of profoundest solitude.

But when we participate in society the scale and number of dialogic interactions multiply exponentially. No activity so thoroughly characterizes culture as the exchange of information, not only through words but through symbols, gestures, numbers, electronic codes and legal tender. This multifarious exchange is not carried on randomly but rather occurs through a huge variety of communicative protocols and structures. In Chapter 5 I describe

> institutions, from nations down to schools and corporations, [which] have communicative systems analogous to the nervous systems of animals. These systems comprise all communicative modes, including the doors, windows and hallways of the architecture, the relationship between floors of a building, the interrelationship of buildings or branches, the vocabulary and structure of professional language (including computer software), the electrical and electronic hardware, the memos and newsletters and data resources, the amount of time available for communication and the overall communicative strategy or tradition.

These structures determine the type of information to be communicated, the speed of communication, the availability of information, the possibility of response. In a more political sense, they also determine the quality of discourse within a given institution, the power inherent in its component departments and its ability to evolve over time. Significant disproportions in the communicative activity of various institutions suggest the presence of "open" and "closed" communicative systems, i.e., systems in which tradition, policy or mere chance has maximized or minimized the flow of information. These channels and mechanisms bear importantly on the success of the institution and the lives of the individuals involved in it. Perspective, confidence, integrity, empowerment, even enthusiasm, depend in large measure on the quality of communicative systems. We will find that open systems, for all their looseness and apparent lack of security, radiate more immediate happiness and possess more potential staying power and substance for evolution than their closed counterparts.

A similar issue operates in the macrocosm of the state. In a healthy democracy, political liberty is infinite, for every positive initiative (invention or business venture or social project) generates a new context of choice. Here each free act is a creative act, and every new victory or achievement for one is a victory or achievement for all. Conversely, in a sick democracy — impoverished or overcrowded or dispirited or too concerned with security — political liberty is a limited commodity granted to one citizen or group only at the expense of the others. Here each liberty gained by an individual or group can be part of a vicious cycle in the erosion of community. Thus the only way to maintain liberty, or to restore it when it has weakened, is through growth — not physical growth so much as growth into new forms of awareness and new avenues of enterprise. Such growth, which can be compared to growth along a frontier, is impossible without open communications and universal access to information.

DIALOGUE AND SELF-TRANSCENDENCE

We come now to the most radical formulation of the idea of liberty. The idealist tradition since Socrates, the great religions and the mystics have taught that the most desirable form of liberty is not a freedom *of* the self but a freedom *from* the self: a transcendence of confining individuality. To some, this is a spiritual quest pursued through meditation and prayer; to others, it is a philosophical exercise requiring concentration and inquiry. This latter exercise is often conducted dialogically. Through dialogic imagining I can posit an "other" (a loved one, a friend, a stranger, even an enemy), focus myself on this other, detail this other until it has spirit, autonomy, volition. To the extent that this is successful, I can achieve an interpersonal understanding impossible under other circumstances; and beyond this I have the opportunity temporarily to look back on myself, as though in a far-off mirror, as a distinct and limited entity.

Dialogic self-transcendence is valuable not only for personal fulfillment but also for artistic achievement and social renewal. Writers, consciously or not, resort to this strategy in developing character, idea, event and place, while actors and actresses enter into dialogic relationships with the parts they play. Without this process we would have dull fancy and tame art. Social possibilities are equally dramatic though less frequently explored. Here dialogic thought allows us to extend awareness not only beyond our personal isolation but also beyond our own gender, age group and ethnicity. With concentration and insight we can project living will into otherwise alien individuals and groups; in so doing we cross barriers that might otherwise cause disaffection or confrontation. Dialogic thinking, which deflects self-interest in the name of interpersonal understanding, becomes in the process a force of social evolution.

THE CONCERNS OF THIS STUDY

The three areas outlined above are the major concerns of this study. But dialogue is too seductive, too allusive, too enchanting an idea to be neatly mapped and delimited into areas. Cross-references abound; familiar themes crop up in unfamiliar places, while insistent associations have forced my attention beyond decorous precincts into a jungle of unauthorized conjectures about language, technology, business, sex, cognition, history, nature and natural science. These I apologize for in advance, with the excuse (not unfamiliar in dialogic thought) that they were not really *my* ideas but rather were dictated by the subject.

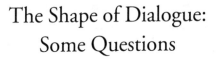

The Shape of Dialogue: Some Questions

What is dialogue? I take the word from its Greek original as "discourse across" — an exchange of meaning "across" *(dia)* some space. Thus dialogue would seem to require

- two or more entities capable of discourse,
- a physical or mental space between these entities, separating them, distinguishing them from each other, and
- a reciprocal exchange of meaning *(logos)* by these entities across this space.

Does this mean that two or more people are necessary for a dialogue? Plato clearly thought not:

Philosophy is the mind's dialogue with itself. *(Theaetetus)*

The mind can dialogue with itself by asking questions and trying to answer them or by setting up two different frames of reference and comparing them; more ambitiously, the mind can examine its own words and premises in order to understand itself or renew its way of seeing the world. Like a nimble wrestler, the mind can thus slip free from the fixed images and rigid values of ideology into an all but limitless diversity of ideas and approaches. Chronically self-examining, the mind can loop back on itself in a lifelong spiral of challenge and response.

What happens in dialogue? The key ingredients are reciprocity and strangeness. By reciprocity I mean a give-and-take between two or more minds or two or more aspects of the same mind. This give-and-take is open-ended and is not controlled or limited by any single participant. By strangeness I mean the shock of new information — divergent opinion, unpredictable data, sudden emotion, etc. — on those to whom it is expressed. Reciprocity and strangeness carry dialogue far beyond a mere conversation between two monolithic information sources. Through reciprocity and strangeness, dialogue becomes an evolutionary process in which the parties are changed as they proceed. This process may be illustrated as follows. Party A begins a dialogue with Party B by stating a view or asking a question. Party B, now in receipt of new information, is changed by it and changed again in formulating a response, becoming B_2; B_2's reply has a similar effect on Party A, and so on:

$$A_2 \rightarrow B_3 \rightarrow A_3 \rightarrow B_4 \rightarrow A_4 \rightarrow B_5 \ldots$$

These changes may be microscopic, but nonetheless their existence marks dialogue as a special kind of communication and a potential avenue of freedom.[2]

Is dialogue an exclusively human phenomenon? Not at all. Any interaction that is reciprocal and open-ended should be viewed as dialogic. I say "should" because by understanding the idea of dialogue too narrowly, we stand to miss the splendid things that nature can teach us about itself and ourselves. Evolution, ecosystems, the human body, the living cell: these are best understood as

---

2. Students of chaos theory and complexity theory will note that if we describe an open-ended dialogue as $A^1 \rightarrow B^1 \ldots A^x \rightarrow B^x$, normal human factors (mood, impulse, time of day, etc.) will cause the level of chaos (i.e., randomness) to rise with

dialogic entities, self-regulating interactions of multiple forces. A sense of this dialogue pervades the work of the great ecologist Aldo Leopold, who writes:

> Modern natural history deals only incidentally with the identity of plants and animals, and only incidentally with their habits and behaviors. It deals principally with their relations to each other, their relation to the soil and water in which they grew, and their relations to the human beings who sing about "my country" but see little or nothing of its inner workings.[3]

Elsewhere Leopold advises us to "think like a mountain": to imitate in our own minds the subtly dialogic reciprocity of an ecosystem.[4] Nature talks and responds to itself, not in words but in eloquent gestures, as minute as the excretion of a hormone, as enormous as the evolution of a species. Nature may not philosophize, but its avowals astound philosophy, just as its creativity dwarfs poetics.

Are dialogic interactions always positive? Yes and no. They're always positive in the sense that they always generate some sort of energy. They shed light on nature and human affairs. Usually this results in growth and progress. But of course dialogue is a form of power, and power of any sort can be misused.

Misused how? By the creation of interactions that look dialogic but actually are not. For example, administrators can use dialogic forms (question and answer, open forum) to disguise their hidden agenda while building an illusion of familiarity and trust. Con-

---

each interchange. Thus dialogue, like the weather, is unpredictable. See Gleick, *Chaos,* pp. 21–31.

3. *A Sand County Almanac,* pp. 209–10. Because editions of the *Almanac* differ from each other in organization, note that this sentence is from the section entitled "Natural History" in the essay called "A Taste for Country," originally not in the *Almanac* but in *Round River.*

4. Ibid., "Thinking Like a Mountain," pp. 137–41.

versely, subordinates can use dialogic forms (protest, networking, the questioning of authority) to create power bases for purely selfish designs. Seen generally, dialogue, like love, is an interaction that quite often inspires excitement and good feelings: in other words, a powerful rhetorical tool that holds danger as well as promise.

Misuse of a less calculated nature characterizes the dialogic reciprocity defined by Gregory Bateson as "schismogenesis" or "progressive differentiation."[5] In such an interaction a verbal initiative on the part of one party (e.g., a boast or a threat) triggers a response that increases differentiation, that is, escalates conflict.

But don't we all carry our own stubborn, subjective views into our dialogues with others? We do indeed. Moreover, as Chaim Perelman and L. Olbrechts-Tyteca point out, we may carry *intentions* that will threaten the progress of the dialogue.[6] Thus selfish motives impede us from realizing the full benefits of dialogic interactions. But equally selfish though more dynamic motives often win out over these. The desire for empowerment through knowledge, the thrill of new experience, the love of learning: these selfish motives can dissolve subjectivity and transform intentionality. The delight of discovery can carry dialogue beyond our daily goals, beyond the rhetoric we use to gain them.

If, as you say, dialogic thinking always transcends fixed perspectives, doesn't that preclude drawing conclusions of any sort? No. The mind regularly sorts through great numbers of alternatives and motives only to emerge with a very limited number of choices and deeds. In learning to think dialogically, we learn to benefit from, rather than be impeded by, the multiplicity of our inner motives. All of

---

5. *Steps to an Ecology of Mind*, pp. 61–72. Also notable in this book is Bateson's recourse to a mode of dialogic ("metalogical") presentation in Part I.

6. *The New Rhetoric*, p. 38. For an illuminating chapter on dialogue and dialectic, see Perelman and Olbrechts-Tyteca, *The New Rhetoric and the Humanities*, pp. 73–81.

us have to act decisively and coherently, but that doesn't mean that we can't *consider* our actions with self-awareness and finesse.

You now have more than once equated free thought with breaking free from single into multiple perspectives. But isn't this also potentially confusing and chaotic? True, here as elsewhere the quest for freedom runs the risk of chaos and anarchy. But the mind that is ready to unbuckle itself from the security of a fixed perspective usually has the savvy to avoid such obvious dangers. Besides, dialogic thought can't be content simply to disentangle itself from other perspectives; it must appreciate their power, distinguish what they have in common, dwell on their points of conflict. Only through these procedures can it conceive of new syntheses.

If dialogic thought is so liberating and effective, why haven't more people followed it? I have already described the immense lure that logical, simple, self-coherent perspectives have on the mind (pp. 3–4), but I haven't said anything yet about the Western social context which in effect produces this lure. Most human endeavors, from road construction to classical philology, from theoretical physics to organized religion, are *progressive:* that is, they evolve by building upon or reacting against what has gone before. Thus you can imagine human enterprise in general as a massive edifice, parts of which are constantly under construction or demolition. In this communal effort the emphasis has always been on simplicity, so-lidity and directness; simplistically put, no one wants structural components that pivot, wobble or vibrate. And thus it is that Western discourse — whether we read it in textbooks, political platforms or learned journals — has taken on a monistic, mecha-nistic tone.

Via institutional psychology, this monistic tone is passed on to the young as *the proper way of thinking.* College courses, textbooks, the vast bulk of the published canon, endorse linear, yea-or-nay thinking. Our ten-year-old children, who have not yet rubbed the stardust out of their eyes, are subjected by their teachers to ruthless barrages of mechanistic logic. From every wing of culture, interest groups advertise themselves in terms of arbitrary assertions and monistic rationales. Even psychiatry, the means by which we might address our own mysterious innerness, regularly resorts to material therapies (drugs) and leans toward reductive explanations of our moods and behavior. The bulk of social discourse, in other words, teaches us that our lives can be understood and conducted linearly, by means of a relatively simple network of yeses and noes. We're taught to suppress the organic multiplicity of our own thinking.

You began by describing dialogic thought as something very sophisticated, and now you call it "organic," which suggests lack of sophistication. Isn't that self-contradictory? It certainly is. But this paradox has been noted by almost all contemporary researchers on creativity and innovation. According to them, the greatest contributions to thought have been made by those individuals most attuned to the chaos in thinking.[7] With this in mind, it follows that formal thought would do well to return now and then to the fountain from which it springs: that it should seek out and embody and convey the abundance and turbulence of live thinking. Such a project, we might imagine, would be a kind of philosophical expedition, a journey from town to wilderness or from land to sea. This journey would offer not only refreshment and delight but also the possibility of discovery and liberation.

---

7. See, for example, Koestler, *The Act of Creation,* Chapters 1–3; May, *The Courage to Create,* Chapter 2; Abraham Maslow, quoted in Rothenberg and Hausman, *The Creativity Question,* pp. 89–90, and my *The Grace of Great Things,* Chapters 2 and 3.

PART ONE

LANGUAGE AND

LIBERTY

2

✎✎✎

The Language of Liberty:
Shakespeare's *Hamlet* as a Book of
Dialogic Tricks

Daily living has a decidedly linear character. By this I mean that life, as it includes getting out of bed, having breakfast, going to work and all the rest, unfolds as a series of single choices — which blouse or tie we put on, which way we turn at the end of the block, where we go to lunch — made from a limited number of alternatives. The workplace actions we take, even the words we use, have in them a singleness implying to others and ourselves that we mean specifically what we are doing or saying and that these words and actions are coherent with others in the past and future. This unitary passage through life, a journey that can be described by a line drawn on a piece of paper through a series of forks and intersections, is underwritten by our value system, which prizes words like "forthright," "frank," "consistent," "coherent" and "integrity." Conversely, we cannot express uncertainty or anxiety or pure confusion about the complexity of things without feeling weak and ashamed.

Yet insight from a variety of sources — science, philosophy, psychology, history, even occasional experiences of our own — suggests that all this is an illusion. Physiologically, each of us is a concatenation of over a trillion cells, changing at the rate of millions a day, making up nerves and glands and organs of whose complex daily business we are largely unconscious. Psychologically, we are oceans of potential thought, feeling and action, shaped by past experience yet constantly interacting and renewing on levels of which we are at best partially aware. Socially and politically, we inhabit a world of unspoken premises, hidden dangers, subtle contradictions and quiet intractabilities, a world where nothing is ever quite what it seems to be, a world whose muscular realities warp and attenuate our values. Stretching out vastly beyond the human world is the biosphere, enormous and spine-chillingly beautiful, a live medium that gave us being and now is hostage to our power, an embracing presence so subtly interactive that despite our vaunted science, we cannot predict its cycles of heat and cold. And even beyond the biosphere, dwarfing it, is the cosmos, an inscrutable configuration of energies in endless space and time.

While we see and move linearly, we are actually in the midst of another life, multidimensional and oceanically rich. Sometimes this other life makes itself visible to us, in a natural event or family tragedy or rite of passage or sudden flow of emotion. But mostly it remains hidden, obscured by the rush of our daily affairs, our lack of practice in focusing on it, our shyness in confronting its vastness. Yet this obscurity does not annul its power. Indeed, the multiple dimensions of our lives often exert a power over us that is directly proportional to our ignorance of them.

Liberty, conversely, would seem to inhere in the ability to bring to awareness and have discourse with as many dimensions of life as possible. The free mind, the dialogic mind, listens and speaks on several levels and in several languages. Not all of these languages are verbal; some are symbolic or sensuous. Not all of these languages are logical; some are passionate, absurd or preposterously funny. Finally, none of these languages offers much hope of conclusiveness; some are made of disconnected images, others of interrupted whispers. We look to these languages not for the resolution of life's issues but rather as a means of understanding what the issues are and of facing them as free people. But what is the medium of enfranchisement, and what language does a dialogic mind speak with itself?

It may come as a surprise if I suggest that an effective dialogic language not only already exists but has been available to most of us for years. Such a language is the eloquence of our forebears, as preserved in great literature. And it is because of the liberating potential of this language, perhaps, that generations of readers have felt at ease with the very idea that such literature is "great."

The language I am about to discuss is not so much a language of words — though it usually is expressed in words — as a language of tropes, or rhetorical figures, passed down to us from classical antiquity as part of the *trivium* of language arts (see Chapter 1). Many of these figures are more or less what you might expect: tricks to give emphasis or excite the audience. Others, however, have the capacity to open up the mind in striking ways. I will comment on five of these, drawing my examples from a familiar source, Shakespeare's *Hamlet*.

PARADOX

Questioned by Rosencrantz and Guildenstern about his strange behavior, Hamlet responds,

> I have of late — but wherefore I know not — lost all my mirth, forgone all custom of exercises; and indeed it goes so heavily with my disposition, that this goodly frame, the earth, seems to me a sterile promontory; this most excellent canopy, the air, look you, this brave o'erhanging firmament, this majestical roof fretted with golden fire, why, it appeareth nothing to me but a foul and pestilent congregation of vapors. What a piece of work is a man! How noble in reason! how infinite in faculties! in form and moving, how express and admirable! in action, how like an angel! in apprehension, how like a god! the beauty of the world! the paragon of animals! And yet to me what is this quintessence of dust? (II.ii)

Leaving plot and character aside here, consider this passage as a mental exercise for the audience member or reader. We are presented with a paradox, an apparent contradiction in terms. In linear terms, the air, a "brave o'erhanging firmament, this majestical roof fretted with golden fire," cannot be "a foul and pestilent congregation of vapors," and man, "the beauty of the world," cannot be a "quintessence of dust." What Shakespeare is asking us, almost requiring us, to do is move beyond linearity to a double perspective in which we *simultaneously* recognize the value of life and consider life worthless. Like many other Shakespearean paradoxes, this passage challenges us to bring to consciousness the multileveled structure of human experience, the dangerous richness of human emotion.

Even more is at work here. Considering the passage from the point of view of the history of ideas, we find two important European thought systems at odds with each other in Shakespeare's lines: the *contemptus mundi* (contempt for the world) tradition, common to both Catholicism and Anglicanism, versus the humanistic anthropocentrism and optimism born with the Italian Renaissance. Both of these ideologies were common in Shakespeare's milieu, and most educated people felt the stress between them. Each system seemed to offer a special kind of truth, yet each wholly contradicted the other. In throwing these two truth systems together, Shakespeare provokes the members of his audience to consider the contradiction inherent in their own perspectives. He asks them to transcend ideology and recognize that truth is not linear but rather complex and multiform.

DOUBLE-ENTENDRE

Immediately after calling humanity a "quintessence of dust," Hamlet continues,

> Man delights not me — nor women neither, though by your smiling you seem to say so.

Here is a play on the verb "to delight." Hamlet uses the word in its general sense as "giving pleasure"; but when he sees Rosencrantz smile, he suspects that his friend has given the word a more specific, sensual spin ("giving *erotic* pleasure"). Devices like this occur often in Shakespeare; *Hamlet* in particular is rich in puns and other forms of double-entendre. The effect of this figure is, like that of paradox, one of compounding perspective. Consciousness is taken by surprise and split into two levels, one conventional and one unconventional. The conventional level is usually quite harmless, while the unconventional level is rich in sensual or satiric power. Double-entendres shock their audience out of both linguistic complacency (the sense that a given word has only one meaning) and moral complacency (the trust in polite, business-as-usual social relationships). They thus undermine simplistic interpretations and complicate our experience of literature and life.

METAPHOR

Hamlet holds out a recorder to Guildenstern and asks him to play some music. When Guildenstern declines ("I know no touch of it, my lord . . . I have not the skill"), Hamlet answers angrily,

> Why, look you, now, how unworthy a thing you make of me! You would play upon me, you would seem to know my stops, you would pluck out the heart of my mystery, you would sound me from my lowest note to the top of my compass; [*holds up recorder*] and there is much music, excellent voice, in this little organ, yet cannot you make it speak. 'Sblood, do you think I am easier to be play'd on than a pipe? (III.ii)

Literary metaphors are usually like swift brushstrokes, providing momentary images and building the tone and/or theme of the work they inhabit. They are meant to draw attention not to themselves but to the subject they describe. Here, however, Shakespeare takes a comparison (Prince Hamlet: recorder) and prolongs it until it becomes an event in itself. The metaphor is unpleasant and strangely evocative. Hamlet is upset with Guildenstern for spying on him, prying into his secrets. He compares himself to an instrument Guildenstern wishes to play. In the context of Hamlet's Danish court, where spying and manipulation go on incessantly, the metaphor suggests the falseness of polite appearances and the reality of a social context in which people use their fellows as instruments or tools. The audience members are challenged to rework their own idea of social reality in order to discover whether it contains such an abusive context itself.

IRONY

Having decided to get rid of Hamlet, King Claudius packs him off on a ship to England, with a note (carried by Rosencrantz and Guildenstern) to the English king requesting Hamlet's immediate execution. On board, Hamlet discovers the treachery and impulsively forges a new commission, which he later describes as

> An earnest conjuration from the King,
> As England was his faithful tributary,
> As love between them like the palm might flourish,
> As peace should still her wheaten garland wear
> And stand a comma 'tween their amities,
> And many such like "as's" of great charge, —
> That on the view and knowing of these contents,
> Without debatement further, more or less,
> He should those bearers put to sudden death,
> Not shriving time allow'd.
>
> (V.ii)

Hamlet's note is ironic in three ways. First, it is a loaded text that immediately destroys its own bearers. Second, its gracious "conjuration" from the powerful Danish king to his English tributary conveys the rather ungracious threat of international violence should the English king fail to comply. Third, Hamlet's assumed writing style, so stately yet so deadly, parodies the dishonest political rhetoric characteristically employed by his murderous uncle Claudius.

What is the mental effect of these ironies? Something similar to the effects of paradox and metaphor. The ironies thwart our desire for a linear, monistic interpretation of discourse. Instead, they force us to confront a pair of contradictory realities: one reality in which language is ingratiating, another reality in which the same language is sinister. Momentarily, our minds are startled out of their unitary perspective into a world of multiform experience.

AMBIGUITY

Take Hamlet's overall position. Though after Act III he is certain that Claudius has murdered King Hamlet, he never can decide quite what sort of revenge is justified. Take our view of the play as a whole. Most readers are doubtful as to whether Shakespeare wants them to endorse Hamlet's behavior or impugn it. These ambiguities are clearly part of Shakespeare's intention; they are part of the play's greatness. They give both Shakespeare's hero and his audience a contoured, four-dimensional view of experience, a view amenable to multiple attitudes and subject to evolution in time. This ambiguous tone is strikingly similar to that of real-life crises, in which individuals must bear permanent responsibility for decisions made under pressure. Pondering such decisions, we sometimes feel paralyzed by the number of factors to be considered and the possible consequences of action. *Hamlet* affords us a considered, nonthreatening view of this psychic reality. *Hamlet* is a window into the dizzying multiplicity of experience.

Shakespeare adds to this sense of multiplicity by enriching his character population to include six major roles — Hamlet, Claudius, Gertrude, Polonius, Ophelia and Laertes — more than in any other of his plays except *King Lear*. Each of these characters is equipped with a different body of information about the events in progress; each has a uniquely individual view of what goes on. Shakespeare further complicates things by having Hamlet feign madness and Ophelia actually go mad; in so doing he adds two bizarrely different perspectives to the variety that is already on stage. Together with important lesser roles like Horatio, Rosencrantz/Guildenstern and the Ghost, this variety of perspectives gives the play a strikingly dialogic tone. We are made aware of the enormous number of possible human responses to a given word or action. We are reminded of the different voices — asserting, complaining, accusing, seducing, haunting — that can speak in a single soul.

LANGUAGE AND MIND

All this may remind you of the quiet rush of exhilaration students sometimes feel while reading a good work of fiction or listening to a good lecture about literature. This special excitement brought on by literary art is not the shock of new information; rather, it is that our minds are being taught new tricks, maneuvers that are liberating and delightful. The "tricks" taught by the examples from *Hamlet* all involve a kind of stretching of the mind: expanding the awareness to include multiple perspectives and allow for discordant inner voices.

You may respond that this expansion and liberation are only temporary, that the stunts our minds are taught by good literature apply to literature only. True enough; but is there *any* form of liberation, physical, mental or religious, that is permanent unless it is practiced painfully every day and expanded to include the full personality? It is up to the reader to realize that the dialogic wisdom embodied in literature is applicable across a broad spectrum of nonliterary experience. It is up to the reader to learn it by heart and to make it part of a mental repertoire that is renewed in daily action.

FINAL NOTE: DIALOGUE AND THE
COSMOPOLITAN

The word "cosmopolitan" comes from the Greek *kosmopolites* ("world citizen"); it is associated with the Greek-based "sophisticated" (*sophos,* "clever, wise") and the Latin-based "urbane" (*urbanus,* "of the city"). "Cosmopolitan" is a political word implying transcendence of the narrower limits of politics: local fads, provincial fears. To be cosmopolitan is to be at ease in many situations and with many different sorts of people.

The dialogic mind is cosmopolitan in terms of ideas. It accepts the premise that a given idea or experience can be viewed from a variety of perspectives and that while some of these various perspectives may be mutually complementary, others may disagree with each other. The dialogic mind derives its sophistication, its play of irony and excitement, from accepting this variety and stress.

On Two
Victorian Tiles

One Sunday afternoon in 1994, glancing down at a curio-laden table at Lane County's Piccadilly Flea Market, I suddenly found myself transfixed by the steely eyes of William Gladstone. The formidable Victorian, momentarily as real as life, regarded me from a counter tile, onto which his photographic image had been transferred a hundred-odd years ago by some mass-market ceramics works catering to middle-class households. On a tile next to him, faithful in art as in life, was his wife of fifty-eight years, Catherine Glynne.

I bought the tiles and drove home, wondering along the way what British cook in his or her right mind would have set a pot of potatoes down on the prime minister. My wife, Michaela, resolved this for me when I showed them to her a few minutes later: "Look how yellowed and lined Mrs. Gladstone is. They must have put all the pots on *her!*" This gender-political interpretation impressed me so much that I still can't glance at the tiles without thinking impulsively that one of them has been privileged and one exploited (see Figures 1 and 2, following p. 84).

Was my wife right? It hardly matters. Her interpretation was penetrating enough to convey authority in and of itself. And this may be said of interpretation in general. Because interpretation is born of conviction and expresses itself through verbal art, it can carry a social force that is quite independent of its factual accuracy. It can expand or diminish its subject, or reinvent it altogether.

This power is evident in one of the most ambitious interpretive enterprises in Western history: the Christian appropriation of the Old Testament. Christ asserted that he was the fulfillment of scriptural prophecy, thus opening the way for a vast Christian reinterpretation of the Bible. Later Christian spokesmen, moved by inspiration or desiring to make Biblical meaning conformable to church authority, reinterpreted every major character and event from Adam down to the prophets as a providential preamble to their Redeemer. The Song of Songs, redolent of incense and Eros, was recast as a spiritual allegory; the hero Joseph, exemplar of enlightened Judaism, was reinvented as an anticipatory model of Christ.

This reinterpretation had a profound effect on Western history, not only because it rewrote Western *pre*history in a way that was convenient for Christian authorities but also because it allowed them permanently to avail themselves of the power and sweetness of the Old Testament. To millions of readers even today, the Christian rendering of the Old Testament is revealed truth, while others, including many Jews and Muslims, are somewhat less enthusiastic.

In another episode from early church history, the tables are completely turned. Irked by misunderstandings that had arisen from thirdhand versions of the Old Testament, Saint Jerome retranslated the entire work from the original Hebrew into clear, idiomatic Latin (the Vulgate). This project met with resistance from church authorities, including Saint Augustine, who regarded it as dangerous. Why dangerous? A thirdhand translation of the Bible is nonetheless a holy text, and holy texts are de facto beyond dispute. Put differently, Jerome's new translation constituted a *reinterpretation,* and a reinterpretation creates a multiple and discordant authority that can easily dissolve altogether. Interpretation, the hammer that builds authority, thus can also be the sledge that batters it down.

Similar issues are at work today, particularly in the Interpretation Wars that are exercising so many of our literature professors. The vertiginous and often darkly comic republic of academic discourse now knows no territorial prohibitions: consensus has crumbled, and nothing is more fashionable than the frontal assault on a defenseless text. Interpretation czars in the mold of Heidegger and Foucault build shimmering though questionably habitable palaces of words; deconstructionists bounce along just beyond the pursuit of understanding; and the armies of revision march by night. Long-familiar figures — Shakespeare's Prospero and Caliban, Milton's Lucifer and Eve — parade before us like strangers, in borrowed liveries of class, commerce, gender, psychopathology or whatever else happens to interest the interpreter. In an article entitled "Love Is Not Love," a contemporary scholar, Arthur Marotti, greets us with the revelation that Renaissance lyrics dedicated to the love of the female body and spirit are actually disquisitions on political and economic power.

It is only fair to say that elements of these revisions are fresh and enlightening; but it is necessary as well to note that most of the treatments are jargon-ridden, intellectually narrow and subtly authoritarian. As there seems to be a widespread recognition of the power of interpretation, there seems also to be a general disregard for its considerate use. We are not being enabled to evaluate interpretive systems. Instead we are being offered new systems to submit ourselves to.

All this suggests not only the character of our times but the ambiguous nature of interpretation itself. Like any thought system, like anything we call an "idea," interpretation simultaneously extends and constricts our understanding. It extends our understanding by equipping us to respond to experience; it constricts our understanding by silently negating alternative perspectives. And because it must be a neat fit in order to be convincing, interpretation lacks the abundance and fertility that can accommodate change. You might say that in its quest for efficiency, interpretation forgoes the diversity and redundancy characteristic of living forms and creative thought.

Not that interpretation always *achieves* efficiency. Much of it, as we all know, is murky and contorted. I mean instead that most interpretation, in deference to Western professional tradition and much of Western thinking in general, involves the compulsive effort to close a case, to cork the genie in the bottle.

But what is the alternative? Deconstructive, absurdist fulminations, which have occupied us in fits and starts ever since the Greek Sophists, may be valuable as wake-up calls, but they have little staying power. They do nothing for the human experiences that are so universal and so personal that we deny them at our lives' peril. Is there a middle course between the authoritarian and the absurd? Plato addressed this question directly when, in the *Parmenides,* he attacked both authoritarian and absurdist models of thinking as "the One and the Many" but implied that all thought was a kind of dialogue between them. In our century, Martin Buber and Hans-Georg Gadamer, among others, have developed similar syntheses. All suggest that the healthy mind allows, even encourages, the constant flux between absolute and relative, and that fixed positions or interpretations can only be appreciated in terms of their opposites or alternatives. Thinking of this sort is dialogic. It takes unto itself and even derives energy from the contradictions and ambiguities of human experience. And it imitates inner processes as well. More than any other form, dialogue accommodates the paradox, ambiguity, randomness and conflict that characterize the living mind at work. More than any other form, dialogue imitates the multifariousness, disorder and creativity of live thinking.

As I suggested in the previous chapter, dialogic thinking forms the structure of much great art and thought. It is readily apparent in Montaigne's self-questioning, in Goethe's sense of contrariety and paradox, in the vast character galleries of Chaucer, Balzac and Dickens and in Hegel's astute comment that tragedy is the conflict "between right and right." The Russian thinker Mikhail Bakhtin discovers in many modern novels the dialogic stresses that function as the reader's reeducation for life in society.[8] Dialogue relieves the tension between mind and experience; it eases the stress between consciousness and time.

How can dialogic thinking help me to reconcile myself with Mrs. Gladstone's tile? Simply by opening up new perspectives. I can see Mrs. Gladstone's kitchen duty, if indeed she did it, as a cook's compliment rather than a patriarchal insult. I can see it as bringing her image comfortably into the heart of daily practice and family life, while Mr. Gladstone, isolated in his male authority, was denied this privilege. I can remember the history of nineteenth-century British manufacture, noting the decline of concern for harmony between form and function that ultimately resulted in rather tasteless items like the Gladstone tiles. I can muse on how the tiles got here from England, and on the number of household dramas that their dignified countenances have beheld from counters or walls. And I can look far back to my childhood in mid-century, when objects like the tiles still clustered, as treasured possessions, in the china cabinets of my grandparents.

By thinking in this way, I can free the tiles, or any object or idea, from the prison of a fixed perspective and see them, momentarily, for what they are: things apart from me and my interpretive priorities, the subjects of multiple dimensionality and independent character.

---

8. Bakhtin, *The Dialogic Imagination,* p. 234.

3

❧❧❧

The Liberty
of Ideas

How can we understand the "truth" about a being, idea or event? For most Westerners the answer would be to analyze it, find out what makes it distinct, grind it down to its simplest components. Western philosophy and its more recent offshoot, social science, have largely followed this reductive method of interpretation. So do all of us, when a child asks us for a definition, or when we collaborate with others in the workplace, or when we are forced, during some personal crisis, to find the root of a problem. It is an indisputably useful way of thinking, because it produces communicable results that can be tested against experience. But it is not the only valid means of interpreting things or answering questions — or even of asking them.

Take this example. A tree, according to the third edition of the *Columbia Encyclopedia,* is a "perennial woody plant with a single main stem (the trunk) from which branches and twigs extend to form a characteristic crown of foliage." The encyclopedia entry proceeds to elaborate on this sentence. Yet what do I think of when I muse about trees? I think of them as primary engines in the renewal of the biosphere, as tangible images of beauty, as symbols of stability and fertility, as sources of delicious and sometimes forbidden fruit, as natural birdhouses, as fountains of nature refreshing towns and cities, as singers and dancers in the wind, as brooding congresses in the wilderness, as messengers of symmetry, as natural tranquilizers, as shelters from the rain, as ominous, unforgiving barriers to young sledders, as sun-drenched temples condoning hilarities of children, as rooms whose green ceilings shade the liberties of lovers, as untranslatable presences in dreams . . .[9]

I leave the paragraph unfinished because ideas as profound and intimate as "tree" are always unfinished, evolving, inscrutably interwoven, alive. You cannot package and distribute living ideas. You cannot manage them; *they manage you.* To understand a subject is not to cut it down to size but to expand into it. To interact

---

9. In Chapter 7 I quote a similar passage about trees by Martin Buber. I had not read or heard of the Buber passage before writing my own, and was so struck by the coincidence that I decided to use both of them at different points in my text. For purposes of immediate comparison, here is Buber's version:

I contemplate a tree.

I can accept it as a picture: a rigid pillar in a flood of light, or splashes of green traversed by the gentleness of the blue silver ground.

I can feel it as movement: the flowing veins around the sturdy thriving core, the sucking of the roots, the breathing of the leaves, the infinite commerce with earth and air — and the growing itself in its darkness.

I can assign it to a species and observe it as an instance, with an eye to its construction and its way of life.

I can overcome its uniqueness and form so rigorously that I recognize it only as an expression of the law — those laws according to which a constant opposition of forces is continually adjusted, or those laws according to which the elements mix and separate.

I can dissolve it into a number, into a pure relation between numbers, and eternalize it.

Throughout all this the tree remains my object and has its place and its time span, its kind and condition.

But it can also happen, if will and grace are joined, that as I contemplate the tree I am drawn into a relation, and the tree ceases to be an It. The power of exclusiveness has seized me.

This does not require me to forego any of the modes of contemplation. There is nothing that I must not see in order to see, and there is no knowledge that I must forget. Rather it is everything, picture and movement, species and instance, law and number included and inseparably fused.

with living ideas you need a mode of understanding, a method of interpretation, that is open, generous, forgiving, unpunctuated — a liberty of ideas. Such a liberty, I think, exists in cultures that have not been forced down the relatively narrow avenues of literacy and technology. Such a liberty was also, though for a limited time and to a limited number of people, the province of Western art. To describe it I must go back to the Renaissance.

ERASMUS, RABELAIS AND THE IDEA OF COPIA

The rhetorical term "copia" ("abundance," "plenty") was employed by Roman writers (Cicero, Quintilian) to describe a special virtue of great literature: its enthralling, overwhelming richness in terms of detail, variation and figures of speech.[10] This richness was to them an essential aspect of verbal invention, whether for a politician trying to convince an assembly or for a poet enchanting an audience with a story of heroes. In the Renaissance the notion of copia resurfaced in the work of the Dutch humanist Desiderius Erasmus, whose textbook *De duplici copia verborum atque rerum (On Abundance Both of Words and of Ideas)* became required reading in many European and English schools.[11] An acknowledged master of Latin prose, Erasmus sought to pass on the key to eloquence by describing in detail the verbal means of *expanding on the implications of a single idea.* Early on he gives a demonstration — an expansive set of variations on the theme "I enjoyed your letter":

---

10. See, for example, Cicero, *De oratore,* XXX.xxi.125, and Quintilian, *Institutiones oratoriae,* Book X. For a detailed treatment of literary copia in the Renaissance, see Cave, *The Cornucopian Text,* Chapter 1.

11. On the immense literary and cultural influence of *De copia,* see Donald B. King and H. David Rix's introduction to their edition of Erasmus, *On Copia of Words and Ideas,* pp. 6–8.

Your letter has delighted me very much. In a wonderful way your letter has delighted me; in an unusually wonderful way your letter has delighted me . . . Your epistle has cheered me exceedingly. In truth by your epistle I have been exceedingly cheered. Your note has refreshed my spirit in no indifferent manner. By the writing of your humanity I have been refreshed in spirit in no indifferent manner. From your most pleasing letter I have had incredible joy. Your paper has been the occasion of an unusual pleasure for me. From your paper I have received wondrous pleasure. What you wrote has brought me the deepest delight. From what you wrote the deepest joy has been brought me. . . .[12]

And so on for pages. Pompous, artificial, excessive, grotesque, dizzying, maddening, ludicrous, even self-satirical? Erasmus probably intends it that way. His goal here is not to delight readers but to convey forcefully the enormous vitality of language and its potentially hypnotic power.

Erasmus practiced what he preached. His famous diatribe, the *Praise of Folly (Moriae encomium),* is a huge set of variations on a single theme. His narrator, a female figure named Moria, advances the idea of folly from a variety of angles — now philosophical, now funny, now satirical, now religious — thus delivering copia on an immense scale. The *Praise of Folly,* with its plentiful and playful articulation of a living idea, implies something quite startling about copia: *that copia can be not only a way of expressing things but also a way of discovering and seeing things.* Might not a special kind of power inhere in the observer who is able to study a subject from every possible angle? Erasmus, however, stopped short of this. A pious Christian with a keen sense of decorum, he was not amenable to the revolutionary consequences that such a philosophical leap might entail.

---

12. Ibid., p. 39.

Others were less demure. Erasmus' admirer François Rabelais made copia the basis for a theory of education and a philosophy of life. In his most famous work, the *Gargantua,* he launches into a communal drinking scene that is at once an imitation of Erasmus' "I enjoyed your letter" chapter and a quantum leap beyond:

> "Draw!"
> "Pass it over!"
> "Fill it up!"
> "A mixture!"
> "Give it to me without water, like that, friend."
> "Toss me off that glass, neatly."
> "Draw me some claret, a brimming glass."
> "An end to thirst!"
> "False fever, will you not be gone?"
> "God bless me, my dear, I can't get my gullet working."
> "You've caught a chill, old girl."
> "You're right."
> "By St. Quenet's guts, let's talk of drink."
> "I only drink at my own times, like the Pope's mule."
> "And I only drink from my breviary-flask, like a good Father Superior."
> "Which came first, drinking or thirst?"
> "Thirst. For who could have drunk without a thirst in the time of innocence? . . ."
> "As I'm a sinner, I never drink without a thirst, if not a present thirst, a future one. I forestall it, you see. I drink for the thirst to come. I drink eternally. For me eternity lies in drinking, and drinking in eternity."
> "Let's have a song, let's have a drink, let's sing a catch!"[13]

---

13. Translated by J. M. Cohen in Rabelais, *Gargantua and Pantagruel* (Harmondsworth, England: Penguin, 1955), pp. 48–49. Cohen's note to the "breviary-flask" runs as follows: "A breviary-flask . . . seems to have been made after the shape of a prayer-book, for drinking on the sly. Rabelais himself possessed one."

Rabelais diverges from Erasmus' letter format to describe a scene developing in life. He drops Erasmus' elegant Latinity and revels instead in the wealth of wit and image latent in common French speech. Most important, Rabelais lowers the tone of the copia to drinking and drunkenness. This change is symbolic. In chapters that follow, he turns the idea of drinking and drunkenness into the basis of a life philosophy, summed up in the monosyllable "TRINC" (Drink), which, loosely put, amounts to "Drink in all of life; don't worry about being right about things or certain about things; let all of it excite you."[14]

The notion "TRINC" suggests the radical conversion of copia from a literary form to a life art. This life art is "copious" on three related levels:

- Rabelais proposes a "pansophical" learning program that includes not only the arts and sciences but also sports, trades and crafts.
- He rejects the mind/body distinction and sees a continuum of learning and celebration that includes all basic human activities.
- He propounds a philosophy characterized by universal acceptance, enjoyment and affirmation.

This radical message is mimicked and endorsed by the style of Rabelais' masterpiece, which is in effect a copia on copia itself. To underline and embody his omnivorous philosophy, Rabelais creates a great shaggy dog of a book, alternately philosophical and farcical, statesmanlike and satirical, pious and agnostic, epic and obscene. It is a book whose abrupt variations in style and attitude mimic the inconsistencies of human experience and the rich dissonance of human psychology. Thus it is the perfect vehicle for the Rabelaisian message that these inconsistencies and this dissonance

---

14. Ibid., p. 703 (Book 5, Chapter 45).

are to be "drunk in," accepted, enjoyed and fully expressed by the philosophical mind.

MONTAIGNE, SHAKESPEARE

Rabelais' ideas were dangerous, for by encouraging the mind's liberation from all linear doctrines, he suggested a declaration of independence from every form of authority — intellectual, ethical, political and religious. His writings were condemned by the Sorbonne, and though they enjoyed great popularity, they did not inspire a following. When related ideas appeared later in the sixteenth century, they were advanced by writers who were subtler and less affirmative.

While not originally a disciple of Rabelais', Michel de Montaigne achieved late in life a similar attitude toward human experience:

> Our life is composed, like the harmony of the world, of contrary things, also of different tones, sweet and harsh, sharp and flat, soft and loud. If a musician liked only one kind, what would he have to say? He must know how to use them together and blend them. And so we must do with good and evil, which are consubstantial with our life. Our existence is impossible without this mixture, and one element is no less necessary for it than the other.

> When I dance, I dance; when I sleep, I sleep; yes, and when I walk alone in a beautiful orchard, if my thoughts have been dwelling on extraneous events for some part of the time, for some other part I bring them back to the walk, to the orchard, to the sweetness of this solitude, and to me. Nature has observed this principle like a mother, that the actions she has enjoined on us for our need should also give us pleasure; and

she invites us to them not only through reason, but also through appetite. It is unjust to infringe her laws.[15]

Montaigne's *Essays* lack Rabelais' stylistic fireworks and apologetic tone but nonetheless convey a similar attitude toward knowledge. Like Rabelais, Montaigne is omnivorous, intent on appreciating ideas encyclopedically and from every available viewpoint. He rejects consistency, instead endorsing an honest consideration of conflicting ideas:

> There may be some people of my temperament, I who learn better by contrariety than by example, by flight than by pursuit.
>
> Those who make a practice of comparing human actions are never so perplexed as when they try to see them as a whole and in the same light; for they commonly contradict each other so strangely that it seems impossible that they have come from the same shop.[16]

Montaigne uses the cultural diversity inherent in the discovery of the New World as a dialogic means of breaking out of the European moral context and then looks satirically back in upon it, thus comparing the Catholic Inquisition with cannibalistic practices in South America:

> I think that there is more barbarity in eating a man alive than in eating him dead; and in tearing by tortures and the rack a body still full of feeling, in roasting a man bit by bit, in having him bitten and mangled by dogs and swine (as we have not only read but seen within fresh memory, not among ancient enemies but among neighbors and fellow citizens, and what is worse, on the

---

15. From "Of Experience," in Montaigne, *The Complete Essays,* pp. 835, 850.

16. Ibid., "The Art of Discussion," p. 703, and "Of the Inconsistency of Our Actions," p. 239. In the first quote I have changed the translator's "contrast" to "contrariety"; the French is *contrariété.*

pretext of piety and religion), than in roasting and eating him after he is dead.[17]

He sets viewpoints against each other, making his text dialogue with itself:

Here is Pompeius pardoning the whole city of the Mamertines, against which he is greatly incensed, in consideration of the valor and magnanimity of the citizen Stheno, who took the fault of the people upon himself alone and asked no other favor but to bear the punishment alone. Yet Sulla's hosts, who displayed similar valor in the city of Praeneste, got nothing out of it, either for themselves or for others.[18]

He alternates between essayistic commentary and personal revelation to convey the full human shape of ideas. As a whole, his writing suggests to us that the use of multiple perspectives, though dizzying and disconcerting, is central to the philosophical quest. Conversely, Montaigne's work implies that the Western emphasis on coherence and certainty can in fact be a narcotic, putting our minds through psychologically irrelevant exercises that deaden us to ourselves and to experience.

William Shakespeare was a consummate master of copia, as famous speeches by Shylock, Falstaff, Prince Hal, Richard II and Touchstone attest.[19] To appreciate his skill with the simpler aspects of the technique, consider this often-quoted description of England by John of Gaunt in *Richard II:*

This royal throne of kings, this sceptred isle,
This earth of majesty, this seat of Mars,

---

17. Ibid., "Of Cannibals," p. 155.

18. Ibid., "By Diverse Means We Arrive at the Same End," p. 5.

19. See Shylock's famous "Hath not a Jew eyes?" speech in *The Merchant of Venice,* III.1, Hal's banter with Falstaff in *Henry IV, Part I,* II.4, Richard's deposition speech in *Richard II,* III.3, and Touchstone's catalogue of insults in *As You Like It,* V.4.

This other Eden, demi-paradise,
This fortress built by Nature for herself
Against infection and the hand of war,
This happy breed of men, this little world,
This precious stone set in the silver sea,
Which serves it in the office of a wall,
Or as a moat defensive to a house,
Against the envy of less happier lands;
This blessed plot, this earth, this realm, this England,
This nurse, this teeming womb of royal kings . . .

(II.i)

To create this evocation of the native land, Shakespeare ransacks his imagination for diverse metaphors, synonyms and characteristics (throne, isle, earth, seat, Eden, Paradise, fortress, breed, stone, etc.), piling them one on another exhaustively until they completely populate the listener's or reader's mind. The effect of this copia is one of formal brilliance but also one of intimate recognition, because the overflowing multiplicity of the description reminds us of similar multiplicities in the way we think.

Shakespeare also developed the idea of copia in a grander but less obvious way. He could present, within the broad limits of an entire play, a copia in the implications of a single idea. Consider three apparently unrelated scenes from *Hamlet*:

1. Hamlet, feigning madness, throws a barb at Polonius as they chat about the theater:

    HAMLET. My lord, you play'd once i' th' university, you say?
    POLONIUS. That I did, my lord, and was accounted a good actor.
    HAMLET. What did you enact?
    POLONIUS. I did enact Julius Caesar. I was killed i' th' Capitol; Brutus killed me.

HAMLET. It was a brute part of him to kill so capital a calf there.

(III.ii)

2. Having lost her senses, Ophelia sings a song about men and sex:

By Gis, and by Saint Charity,
Alack and fie for shame!
Young men will do't if they come to't;
By Cock, they are to blame.

(IV.v)

3. The Gravedigger (First Clown) tries in a blundering way to explain a legal point to his companion:

For here lies the point: if I drown myself wittingly, it argues an act, and an act hath three branches — it is to act, to do, to perform.

(V.i)

What connects these passages with one another, and with the central theme of *Hamlet,* is that they are all variations on the idea "to act." Polonius has "enacted" — pretended to be — Julius Caesar. Ophelia mournfully evokes young men's propensity for the sex act ("Young men will do't"). The Gravedigger tries unsuccessfully to reason his way into the secret of action. In so doing, each character becomes part of a large yet subtle dialogue, engaged in by most of the main characters, on the subject of human action.[20]

---

20. Trying to pray, Claudius speaks of heaven, which sees an "action" in its "true nature" (III.iii). Later he questions Laertes about his resolve: "What would you undertake / To show yourself your father's son in *deed* / More than in words?" (italics mine). Laertes replies "To cut his throat i' th' church" (IV.vii). Claudius, the First Player and Hamlet himself all develop the negative polarity of the subject, impotence, in significant speeches (III.iii, II.ii). Hamlet's private speeches concern the subject of action, together with its causes and consequences, throughout. He advises the players, "Suit the action to the word, the word to the action" (III.ii) and goes on,

Stretching over the entire play and centering on Hamlet himself, this dialogue includes such famous discourse as "To be, or not to be" (III.i), "O, what a rogue and peasant slave am I!" (in which Hamlet compares himself to an actor, II.ii) and Hamlet's self-accusatory

> Now whether it be
> Bestial oblivion, or some craven scruple
> Of thinking too precisely on th' event —
> A thought which quarter'd hath but one part wisdom
> And ever three parts coward — I do not know
> Why yet I live to say, *"This thing's to do,"*
> Sith I have cause, and will, and strength, and means
> *To do't.*
>
> (IV.iv, italics mine)

Of course the act Hamlet ponders is violent revenge against Claudius. We feel for his uncertainty, perhaps even share it. Yet the play's larger dialogic structure suggests that Shakespeare has more in mind than a single act of violence — that he is philosophically interested in the idea of action and is running it through a full set of permutations; that he wants us to see it from all its sides: pagan, Christian, psychological, sexual, ethical, political, artistic; that he wants us to see the terrible side of the idea and the light side too. Shakespeare's intention in this copious display is not to simplify and conclude but rather to open up the subject in its living complexity: to realize artistically its latent issues. Instead of exploring the idea of action linearly and abstractly, he expands on it dialogi-

---

to them and later to Horatio, discussing the virtue of temperance: the inner mental balance that permits effective action. Hamlet's gibes at the spy-master Polonius develop the thematic contrast between words and actions ("Words, words, words," II.ii); he stabs Polonius, visually symbolizing the thrust of the real through the false; his epitaph for Polonius is "Indeed, this counsellor / Is now most still, most secret, and most grave, / Who was in life a foolish prating knave" (III.iv).

cally and concretely, showing the many ways in which it lives in the mind and thus making it live in the minds of his audience.

This profound understanding of the relationship between copious thinking and the reality of human experience is what gives Shakespeare's mature work its dynamically unfinished character, its untamable mental vigor. His literary strategy allows his text to transcend ideology and live, so to speak, in the freedom *between* ideas rather than in subjection to them. Copious thought also puts Shakespeare in a special position regarding the old conflict between poetry and philosophy. Thinking copiously, Shakespeare combines Dionysian qualities of poetry (plenty, extremes of feeling, contrariety) with Apollonian qualities of philosophy (exhaustiveness, precise description, open-minded scrutiny); he lets us see that to a mature understanding, Apollo and Dionysus contradict yet also necessitate each other. His artful combination of the two produces a text that, like our own world, is emotionally immediate yet haunted with ideas.

THOUGHTS ON COPIA

It is important to notice that the three examples from *Hamlet* quoted at the beginning of the last section are all humorous: Hamlet pulls a verbal prank on the straight man Polonius, Ophelia lapses into the bizarrely obscene oath "By Cock," and the Gravedigger makes a shambles of philosophical analysis. Several generations of scholars blamed Shakespeare for doing this sort of thing: spoiling the tragic dignity of his plays with gags that lowered the tone. But to see these pranks as examples of copia is to understand their real power. Everything, from the civil to the sacred, has its funny side, and if its potential funniness is not acknowledged, an idea cannot be fully shaped in the mind.

.　　.　　.

❧ From Erasmus right on through Rabelais, Montaigne and Shakespeare, we find the copious mind thriving on contradictions and contraries. Can it be otherwise? To think a subject through from every possible perspective is to become aware of points of view that, though they are quite opposed to each other, have substantial claims to validity. Shakespearean drama draws a great deal of its vigor from such oppositions. Shakespeare is a master at setting up opposed character types or tonalities or ideas and leaving his audience in the dynamically charged space between them. We have seen how he juxtaposes the Dionysian with the Apollonian, the humorous with the serious, Renaissance optimism with medieval *contemptus mundi;* notable also is his use of morally opposite characters (for example, Iago and Desdemona in *Othello* and Caliban and Ariel in *The Tempest*).[21]

❧ Readers sometimes ask me to cite examples of the principles I am describing. I normally tend to shy away from this, mainly because in the course of finding an example that supports my ideas, I generally think of two or three that don't. But if you want to see an example of the way in which copia and only copia can describe a life situation, look at the following fictional anecdote.

I have advertised my seaside retreat for rent and stand on its rickety old deck awaiting the arrival of Mr. Wanicky, a prospective renter. He soon arrives, and as he descends from his pickup I notice that he is a portly man, with a gut about the size and shape of a medicine ball. No sooner is Mr. Wanicky on my deck than a rotten two-by-four gives way and he half falls through it, spraining an ankle and ripping his trousers. I feel
    sad, that Mr. Wanicky has hurt himself;

---

21. Norman Rabkin has discussed this phenomenon in two insightful books, *Shakespeare and the Common Understanding* and *Shakespeare and the Problem of Meaning.*

annoyed, that he has let his weight rise to such a deck-endanger-ing level;

relieved, that it wasn't worse;

anxious, about my ability to give him first aid;

worried, that he might sue;

amused, at the irony of the situation;

ashamed, that my deck was in such bad shape;

angry, that I let it get that way;

guilty, that I have injured someone in the course of my quest for profit.

Of course, the narrator does not feel all these emotions at once; but they are present, brooding, ready to come to consciousness. Though each of them has validity, none, of course, expresses the full picture, and it is difficult, in admitting of all of them, to retain the feeling that one is a single, coherent human being. Such is the case with many intense experiences: the mind, like a prism, takes a single event and splits it into a variety of tones and feelings. Copia alone can express this variety, and that is why copia has a unique value in communicating human experience.

∾ Copia suggests a dynamic relationship between the reasoning and unreasoning aspects of the mind. As we have seen, copia is a *reasoned practice,* derived from rhetorical tradition and indulged in quite artfully by writers and speakers. Yet simultaneously, copia is *an appeal beyond reason,* to the unreasonable, even prereasonable dimensions of mind, to the kaleidoscopic, teeming, untranslatable horde of impressions, memories and emotions that coexist with our more linear thoughts and actions. Copia, then, is reason's effort to transcend its own laws, to explore and frolic beyond itself.

∾ Copious thinking seems to me closer to the female than to the male (though indulging in it might well make males more masculine), closer to childhood than to adulthood, to liberal than to conservative, to play than to business, to dream than to waking, to nature than to civilization.[22] Copia is the art of nature.

∽ To think copiously is to recognize previously unadmitted attractions or antipathies to people and pursuits, to question the authority of established truths and reigning idols, to account for unexplained anxieties, to face darkness and the unknown, to dissolve one's own identity in an ocean of diverse experience. To think copiously is to realize that no idea is totally serious, nor totally absurd.

∽ Copious thinking is liberating, but only to the extent that it is generously indulged. People who repress anger or sexuality, or who are unable to laugh at themselves, or who find certain images too terrible to imagine, or who insist on certainty, or who feel strongly that their work must please an authority figure or peer society, or who always feel rushed, or who cannot respect an enemy or a rival, or who have no sense of identification with another gender or culture or age group, are barred from the fullness of copia.

∽ The perspectives of copia include the individual and the communal, the material and the spiritual, the scientific and the poetic, the reductive and the holistic. We may think as lovers, as strangers, as builders-up, as tearers-down, as environmentalists, as technologists, as patriots, as world citizens, as canny politicians, as angry rebels, as satirists, as parents, as children, as wise ones, as clowns. The soul of copia is a kind of mental roundness open to these perspectives and aware of their validity.

∽ Copia, as I have described it, is the most extreme form of dialogic thought. It is inebriating, disorienting and therefore dan-

22. On copia and the female, see Parker, *Literary Fat Ladies,* Chapter 2.

gerous, a philosophical drug that can be addictive. On one level of Shakespeare's play, Hamlet is a prince who cannot decide if or how or when to take revenge for the death of his father; on another level he is a philosophy student dizzied by the stunning variety of truth.

∾   For these reasons, copious thinking is a practice to be used only in special situations: in meditation, in dialogue, in analysis, in daydreaming, in creative art. You cannot listen to a loved one's request for support or see your children about to engorge a mountain of Halloween candy and deliberate on the issue copiously. You cannot be happily adrift in an ocean of interpretations as you enter the voting booth or as you steer your car into a sharp curve on a cliffside road. Moreover, to function at its best, copious thought, generous and self-forgiving, should be balanced or ballasted by rigorous thought, exacting and self-critical.

∾   And followed attentively enough, copious thinking can lead to a new form of conviction. To appreciate a subject from every possible perspective, to make a tour of the interpretive means, is to touch the subject, to walk into it, as one might walk into a house that one has seen only from the outside before. To think copiously about a tree is to be a tree — not so much as to know how a tree feels as to enter the humanity of the tree, the abundance of things that trees mean to people. To understand this is to see that for all its variety, copious thinking is more often empowering than it is destabilizing, for when we are in touch with the heart of things, with their human whatness, we can speak and act from the heart ourselves.

∾   We see differently with each eye, but the mind processes the varying messages into a single apparent image. Thinking copiously is like seeing with many eyes, eyes that often have extremely different points of view. Yet through their unstinting counterpoint a single image takes shape, an image that is neither all of them nor any one of them, an idea as unified in essence as its means are varied.[23]

ᗡᕐ There is a sexiness about this way of thinking, not only because it is open to the sexual overtones and undertones of things but also because of the intimacy and abandon at the heart of the very methodology. Copious thought guards no secret, admits of no pretense, revolts against control in its rush to mingle with ideas and breed with them.

ᗡᕐ Conversely, human sexuality is a kind of copia: a medley of joy, shame, pleasure, pain, light, darkness, assertion, submission, affirmation, denial, privacy, communality, self-gratification, generosity, obliteration, creativity, mystery, revelation. To understand sexuality copiously is never to be dominated by it and never to grow bored with it.

ᗡᕐ Copia is related to the idea of freedom in a number of ways. Copia is liberating

- in its ability to open up the full variety of the mind,
- in loosening the hold of mental bullies like consistency, certainty and coherence,
- in giving individuals a broadened sense of alternatives in interpretation and action,
- in enhancing individuals' appreciation of one another's views and thus opening up dialogue.

ᗡᕐ *Can copious discourse be misused by a subtle rhetorician?* As we will see in the following Interlude, distorted forms of copia can be

---

23. Martin Buber carries this paradoxical reintegration of dialogism with essentialism to its furthest extension: a revelation of God.

used as emblems of institutional power. But in general copia is an experience that energizes rather than intimidates. On top of this, it's hard for a dishonest person to use the sort of copia I've described, because that sort of thinking opens up the full mind, the full person: it's the opposite of concealment, and it mitigates against the goal-driven narrowness of the lie.

⁊   How does Hamlet solve the problem of thought and action? He decides to act *on impulse* and trust in providence:

> Rashly —
> And prais'd be rashness for it — let us know
> Our indiscretion sometimes serves us well
> When our deep plots do pall, and that should teach us
> There's a divinity that shapes our ends,
> Rough-hew them how we will.
>
> (V.ii)

Many readers are satisfied with this decision. But considering its philosophical implications, I think it a kind of unnecessary denial: it rejects the potential for an effective interplay between mind and will. It denies the possibility that a mind may be mature enough to think multilinearly and act linearly — that we can learn the necessity of degrading the multiplicity of our perceptions into the simplicity of our actions. It also ignores the chance that truly artful action can be at once multilinear and effective — the possibility, in other words, that by behaving artfully and creatively, we can put the power of copia into action.

⁊   As it appears in Erasmus, Rabelais, Montaigne and Shakespeare, copia is a characteristically Renaissance event, cousin to other expressions of kaleidoscopic richness: "wonder cabinets" and "wonder chambers" containing varieties of unusual objects, the rise of the modern museum in (among other cities) Prague, Copenhagen and Oxford, the rise of polyphony and the passacaglia in music, the emergence of "variety" as a subject to be discussed in its own right and unusual developments in mannerist art.[24] The frame of mind that produced these phenomena is attracted to encyclopedic inquiry and liberating self-consciousness, but by the same token it is alienated from the spiritual/political certainties of medieval Christianity and from the security of a fixed and communal value system.

This ambiguity between liberation and alienation was to become the basis of the modern consciousness. It spawned two attitudes that continue to dominate Western identity today: the scientific emphasis on limitless inquiry and self-empowerment, and the political ambivalence and moral relativism that are characteristic of the modern intellectual. Where the Western mind gained power, it lost direction; where it gained freedom, it lost identity.

⁊ What happened to literary copia after Montaigne and Shakespeare? Erasmian influence declined, and the rhetorical theory of copia became less available to students. Moreover, literature and literary theory in both France and England established standards of form and correctness that put sharp limits on expansiveness, exploration and innovation in writing. Even more generally, the Western sensibility retreated from the frontier mentality — the distaste for theory and passion for discovery — which could account for the flights of a Rabelais, a Montaigne or a Shakespeare. Leaving such thoughts and writings behind as primitive or unaccountably rough, European wits sought what was for them at once more ethically secure and more stylistically elegant: the neoclassical drama of Racine and Corneille, the sublime numbers of Mil-

---

24. On the origins of the modern museum, see Evans, *Rudolf II and His World.* On Renaissance notions of variety, see Le Roy, *Of the Interchangeable Course of Things,* Shakespeare's characterization of Cleopatra as displaying "infinite variety" (*Antony and Cleopatra,* II.2) and Montaigne, *Essays,* "Of Experience," or my *Mighty Opposites,* Chapter 5.

ton, the rhymed couplets of Dryden and Pope, the reasoned periods of Dr. Johnson and Voltaire. Nineteenth-century romanticism would seem to have opened the doors again for copious thought; in the work of Balzac, Flaubert, Dickens, Melville, Whitman, Tolstoy, Conrad and Joyce, we find a richness reminiscent of the Renaissance. But the twentieth century brought with it new theoretical standards of control and propriety, as well as a schism between belles-lettres and common discourse, which have limited the free flow of literary ideas.

∽ Experience haunts us with its variety. I keep a writer's journal for this book; I quote from the first page, which describes a house I have just moved into:

> B. D.'s house at 1516 L. St., where we arrived in two waves late last month, is a boxlike turn-of-the-century wooden labyrinth designed by Julia Morgan and added on to, probably by someone with kids. A large house, sitting on the hill like a fat brown tabby on its haunches, with seven rooms, two baths and two halls on the second floor alone (two studies included); a forking front-back staircase, a Baldwin grand piano backed up by a harpsichord and pump organ and bizarre native instrument collection, four fireplaces opening onto a single chimney, a seven-doored master bedroom, a jungle of potted plants, a stairwell housing a gallery of ancient family photos, a south-facing deck, a flower-walled patio-cum-spa-and-fishpond complete with bamboo thickets, a cactus garden and a Sloppy Joe loquat tree, into which our cats climb for dramatic standoffs with a furious squirrel; a wet bar gorgeously tiled, a landing loo, four beaten-up stereo sets, a vertical acre of dark paneling, a slew of Turkish rugs, some covering damaged ceilings; an arsenal of graphics ranging from nineteenth-century Persian gardens to Czechoslovakian campaign posters to Klimt's feverish sexuality; multitudinous closets, cabinets and drawers loaded to bursting with family jetsam, dark turnings opening onto darker turnings, an exercise room complete with weights and cross-

country skiing machine; ancient manuscript pages propped up unsteadily on wall moldings, walls of bookspines arranged as solar spectra, a bookcase-top procession of miniature carved elephants, an intelligent piebald stinking Laocoön-faced dog named Yogi, with a penchant for concealing herself on the darkest landing on the off chance that, racing downstairs when one of the kids rings the doorbell, you might fail to notice, step on her and plummet wheeling and flailing to your death against the woodwork below; a hundred surfaces decorated with every variety of curio (goat skull, wolf skull, beer flagons, potsherds, mineral nuggets, fertility icons, demon-chasers and totemic ritual masks, from Turkey, the Holy Land, Bali, Tibet, India), stunning views of the bay, two dozen leaded windows unpropped and ready to bash their panes out in the breeze, antiquated plumbing and wiring, strange built-in boxes covered with cracked brown paint and revealing, when opened, cast iron fixtures from bygone rooms; a master bathroom with a window for convenient observation from the corridor beyond, two museum-quality bathtub showers with dinky tap handles that do the opposite of what they're supposed to as, with the old plastic shower curtains jumping up to goose you (for rising hot air tends to create a vacuum), you try to adjust them; a moldy subterranean Model T–vintage garage housing a '60s VW bug in several hundred pieces and a city garbage can whose aroma must approach the Platonic model of rot; a Squirrel Nutkin scale-model kitchen with a death-dealing superleak gas stove and a final unction fridge, numerous smoke alarms that start shrieking the moment you put bread in the toaster, the air ablur with Yogi's fleas, and a Fauvist kitchen door which, despite its rough-hewn massiveness, seems about to fall off its hinges every time it's touched.

Why the heap of details? They suggest the complexity of a lived-in house, the strangeness of moving into *someone else's* lived-in house. They speak of the variety of moods — awe, fear, anger, delight, annoyance, nostalgia, confusion — that mingle in this complexity and strangeness.

↬ To think copiously is to think with the mind and the body, to have full and intimate contact with experience, approaching that of a wild animal's in nature. Drawn into the universe of an idea, the mind loses its assumed shape, its entangled rationalizations are loosened, the self dissolves, the thinker becomes nobody, the thinker is one with thought.

↬ The vitality of a work of art or system of thought lies in the dialogic interrelationship of its components: in the harmony, discordance and raw friction of its internal elements. These interactions are spiritual, untranslatable, often felt rather than thought out. Their intimate theater is the mind of the beholder. Living thought is beyond words, or rather in the spaces between words and between ideas. But if you take this living pattern and give it to a popularizer or professor, it will get named and cooked; the vital rawness will leave it and will be tame and harmless and easy to communicate. To name an idea is to bury it.

↬ I tend to think copiously about myself, linearly about others; that is, I tend to interpret myself as a full and valid complexity of motives, while I tend to interpret other people's actions within a limited moral grid. Such is the endless tension between self and other.

Dialogic Effects in Renaissance Art

Mind-opening literary tricks such as metaphor, paradox and copia have their counterparts in the visual arts. Anamorphosis was a creative strategy practiced by artists in the Renaissance. Its effect is to force the viewer to interpret the same work of graphic art from two distinct perspectives, thus bifurcating the way in which the mind "reads" visual data. In *Hidden Images,* by Fred Leeman, Joost Elfers and Mike Schuyt, the method is described as follows:

> The system of central perspective not only rationalizes the relationship between objects within a picture, but also establishes a relationship between the viewer and the represented images. Anamorphoses are an extreme example of this subjectivization of the viewing process. The observer is first deceived by a barely recognizable image, and is then directed to a viewpoint dictated by the formal construction of the painting. Indeed, the etymological origin of the word — from the Greek *ana* (again), *morphé* (shape) — indicates that the spectator must play a part and re-form the picture himself.[25]

---

25. P. 9.

Figures 3 and 4 are both by Albrecht Dürer's pupil Erhard Schön. In Figure 3 a strange landscape, when viewed from an extreme righthand or lefthand angle, reveals the recognizable portraits (reading down) of Emperor Charles V, Ferdinand of Austria, Pope Paul III and Francis I. This configuration, plus the iconography (God repelling a Turkish rider, middle left), suggests the year 1534, when Francis I leagued with Suleiman II of Turkey against Charles. Five years earlier Suleiman had besieged Vienna but had been turned back by storms. The woodcut thus reveals itself as a satire of Francis' "un-Christian" behavior.

The second Schön woodcut (Figure 4) is entitled *Aus, du alter Tor* ("Out, You Old Fool"). Here a January-May courtship scene is accompanied by an apparently amorphous flow of lines which, when viewed from a shallow perspective on the left, reveal themselves to be the lovemaking that follows. The hunting scene above plays out the courtship in symbolic terms.[26]

In both cases the *hidden* material — the pictures that must be recovered by our "shaping again" — is volatile (political satire, sexuality). Anamorphosis thus performs for the mind's *visual* faculty what Shakespeare's devices perform for the mind's *linguistic* faculty: it splits consciousness into more than one perspective, reveals a dynamic and dangerous new avenue of cognition. Through anamorphosis, as through Shakespeare's devices, we realize that perspectives are relative, that there is no single proper attitude toward a work of art. This realization opens us up to new ways of seeing.

The idea of abundance or copia is apparent in the work of the sixteenth-century Flemish painter Pieter Brueghel. Taking a single category, children's games, he runs through a dizzying variety of permutations (Figure 5) which effectively imitate the copious descriptions of the humanists (Rabelais spent a whole chapter of

26. Ibid., pp. 11–13.

Gargantua listing children's games). In another painting, *The Blue Cloak* (*Netherlandish Proverbs,* Figure 6), Brueghel enlarges on a theme that had been memorialized by Erasmus.[27] In both cases the effect is striking and paradoxical. The viewer is simultaneously impressed by the multiplicity of human invention and by the diversity of human folly. Like his literary forebears, Brueghel makes a simple response to his work impossible.

An equally radical example of copious thought in art is the work of the mannerist Giuseppe Arcimboldo, who was court painter and revel-master for the Holy Roman Emperor Rudolf II in Prague. Mannerist theory stipulated that the appearance of a painting should be subjugated to the expression of an inner idea. The idea that Arcimboldo is conveying in the paintings depicted in Figures 7 and 8 could be translated as "the copious varieties of imperial power."[28] In Figure 7 the emperor is seen as Vertumnus, a Roman god of nature and change. The strange interplay between human face and botanical collection suggests the emperor's transformation, qua emperor, from a human being into something superhuman: a natural force. The composite image of vegetables and fruits implies the variety and abundance of imperial power. While Figure 7 is a stand-alone, Figure 8 is one of a four-part series depicting the elements earth, water, air and fire. Fire, shown here, is a fierce and angry being composed of flames, fuses, armor and weaponry. The symbolic message is that imperial power, creative and abundant as it may be, can also be militant, furious, unforgiving. The message of the entire series is that imperial power can change swiftly and completely to respond to any circumstance.

Though these symbolic postures are reminiscent of literary copia, and probably partake of the same creative attitude, their

---

27. See Erasmus, *Adages.*

28. For an analysis of these paintings and ideas, see Thomas DaCosta Kaufmann's "The Allegories and Their Meaning."

message is diverted, even perverted, from the messages offered by Rabelais, Montaigne and Shakespeare. Literary copia subverts the authority of monist systems; it invites the mind to play, explore and consequently grow. Imperial copia, however, awes and intimidates, positing state power as a superhuman construct mysteriously linked to nature and divinity. Lavishly, almost voluptuously, literary copia offers the promise of individual liberation. Imperial copia, in a sinister and frightening way, points toward the enfranchisement of authority.

Arcimboldo's artful publicity stunts on behalf of his emperor were in vain. A neurotic recluse who vastly preferred art to life, Rudolf neglected the responsibilities of rule and was ultimately deposed by his brother Matthias. Dispersed in the Thirty Years War, Arcimboldo's paintings were not brought together for a major display until the 1980s.

4

The Dialogue of Invention

One of the most mysterious elements in the creative process is the ever-changing relationship between artisan and artifact. Though that relationship might seem a simple one (as in artisan = maker, artifact = thing made), it is in fact a subtly reciprocal process, in which the artifact, once begun, takes on an independent identity that influences the artist's creative strategy and technique. Artistic creation can thus be viewed as a cybernetic or feedback interaction that continues until the work is complete. It can also be seen, from a different theoretical perspective, as an example of the so-called hermeneutic circle: interreactive relationship between observer and observed.[29] In this study, however, I wish to treat it under a topic heading at once more general and less technical than cybernetics or hermeneutics. I wish to discuss the creative process as a form of dialogue.

This metaphor springs out of my own life experience. For the last five years of the 1980s I was at work on *The Grace of Great*

---

29. On cybernetics, the classic sources are Norbert Wiener's *Cybernetics* and *The Human Use of Human Beings.* On the hermeneutic loop or circle, see the Fourth Interlude.

Things, a book on the theory of creativity and innovation. In the spring of 1990, when that book was about to appear, the English Department and Humanities Center at the University of Oregon were kind enough to let me offer a course on the subject matter that I had been exploring. Because I wanted my students to be as variously expressive as possible and to think about the course material in as many different ways as possible, I asked them all to keep journals — work diaries completely for their own private use. I suggested that they express their aspirations in these journals, admit their doubts, assert their dignity, confess their errors, describe the process of daily life, make notes from their reading, and in general bring their human complexity out of silence and into contact with the challenges of the course. Halfway through the term, it occurred to me that I should be keeping a journal too — not a journal concerning the course but rather a medium for communicating my own creative or uncreative impulses.

I sat down at the computer and wrote:

April 14, 1990

10:40 A.M., brilliant Saturday morning, Eugene the past few days looking like late May or June, except for the many empty-blossomed or green-fuzzed limbs. Air almost soupy with pollen, driving many who have allergies (including my friend Steve Shankman) mad. In my office, 372 PLC, U of Oregon, my writing place of many years, since the middle '70s, when it became Action Central for a book on Shakespeare, down through the record streak of rejections on the time book, and then a pathological burst of writing, 1985–1989, catalyzed by the appearance of a word processor. In '89 this pace slowed down to nickel-and-dime work on articles, unschedulable revisions on *The Grace of Great Things* and other small items. I felt that I needed rest. I felt shocked, almost afraid of what I had said in my last book and spiritually exhausted by it. I was depressed by four months last year that included a car crash, my son Teddy's pneumonia and the death of my Aunt Ruth. The whole idea of rest, symbolized during the rainy winter by the simple image of stretching out somewhere warm in the daytime and going to sleep, was always in my mind, and I was unsure whether I would ever want the strain of writing a full-length book again. Still am.

But if I do, it may be a novel like this: I want to expand on the consequences of a creative act. The fictional act will be a book written by a college professor, so there will be an autobiographical component. The "Book" will be a creative act in two ways: 1) because books always are, 2) because our professor's book will be iconoclastic and direct in ways that most books aren't. Bk will meet with stock responses and kooky responses; the latter will power the plot.

I won't bore you with much more of this.[30] The point of it all is that before beginning my journal, I had not known how much I wanted to write a novel or how strong an idea I had of what I wanted to write. The first page of the journal, with its framing reference to the weather, its historical fix, its complaints and its wishfulness, somehow gave me the resolve *to think in words about what I wanted to do.* In other words, the journal as artifact had influenced me as author.

I continued the journal on an almost daily basis for five weeks, focusing on my projected novel, introducing characters and getting to know them, chatting about style, flirting with plot elements. Via the journal I was creating a dim, impressionistic landscape, the world into which the novel would be born. One day, this world became real enough for me to feel myself able to enter it:

---

30. This journal has been published in full as *A Writer's Journal: 1990–92* by the Voyager Co. (New York, 1993) as part of an "expanded book" (Hypertext computer disk) that also includes the novel *Book*.

This morning for the first time I felt *inside* this novel, in the position not of someone who invents characters and events but of someone who describes things already present but as yet shadowy.

When, in the middle of May, I finally wrote the first pages of the novel, it was in the journal that I began them. Then, using the Block command in WordPerfect, I transferred them into a new file with its own name.

It soon occurred to me that keeping the journal in memory might be of great help in writing the novel. The journal, I thought, could be a kind of literary workshop or studio; as such it could dampen the nervousness likely to build up in me during tense or difficult sections. I saw the journal, as I had seen the novel, as a kind of mental locale; but while the locale of the novel was full of vigor and tension, the locale of the journal was relaxed, informal, sloppy, forgiving: a place to visit before getting into the novel each day, a place to retreat to after temporary defeats or risky adventures.

I continued this practice throughout the first draft of the novel and beyond. The journal became many things for me: a confessional, a chronicle of health, mood and weather, a commentary on how work was proceeding, a repair shop into which I could drag damaged pieces of text and work on them before reinstalling them in the novel; a committee room for discussing plans, a notebook for phone numbers, messages and shopping lists; a forum for trying out ideas, a storehouse for potentially helpful facts and odd ideas, a lounge, a locker room, a consoling listener, a jesting partner, an intimate companion. I found that using it not only drew me swiftly and deeply into the novel but also helped me get rid of distracting details and anxieties that otherwise would have plagued me from within. The journal, in effect, was teaching me how to write, at least to the extent that keeping it allowed me to recapture almost daily the feelings of excitement and engagement I had sometimes felt before when writing well.

Rather than slowing work on the main text, journal-keeping actually seemed to speed it up. By late summer the novel was off to a publisher. Over the next two years, until the book actually appeared, I continued the journal, which was helpful in revising, dealing with readers' responses and, most of all, facing the disappointment and uncertainty of a rejection in the spring of 1991.

What has all this got to do with dialogue? Simply this: writing is a dialogic process. The moment you have committed a sentence to paper, the paper declaims that sentence back to you, as another person might. The assembled letters on the page are other than you: yours, yet not wholly yours, for by writing them in *language* you have entered a forum that is shared by your whole culture. As your manuscript grows, your relationship with it becomes more complex. Now it is no longer a simple statement but a literary organism whose complexity, implication, ambiguity, delight or trouble you. Rationalizing, you may assert that it is under your control, but you forget the controls that it exerts on you: the fact that as a writer you are simultaneously a reader, being pulled and pushed by what you have done.

This pull and push can take dramatic turns. Sometimes a writer can, day after day, fall into his or her text with the passion and abandon of a lover; sometimes, though, the text becomes a monster, a bone-freezing Medusa the very sight of which saps potency and muzzles inspiration. This latter phenomenon is the dreaded writer's block. Writer's block, a sort of literary stage fright, generally manifests itself as a *phobia for the text.* The dialogic give-and-take between text and writer has touched off in the latter some deep-seated anxiety or fear; this anxiety or fear reaches consciousness as a distrust of the manuscript or distaste for writing. The text, which had been part of an intimate interaction, grows foreign, unfriendly; the dialogue is interrupted.

Look at writer's block this way, and you are reminded of some of the more obviously dialogic interactions in life: a love affair that is cut off abruptly when it touches a neurotic chord in one of the lovers; a relationship between a doctor and a psychiatric patient who, suddenly struck with dread at the self-discoveries he or she is making, dismisses the doctor. Each of these cases involves a failure in dialogue. If the lovers were accustomed to sharing each other's feelings, they might have gotten to the root of the problem; if the patient were accustomed to telling the psychiatrist everything, the doctor could have spoken to the cause of the patient's dread.

This brings me, as you might imagine, back to journal-keeping. For me, the writer's journal opened up a *third dialogic avenue,* a channel that eased my own communications with the main text by mediating between it and me and by allowing me to express my distractions and upsets. Eclectic, forgiving and thoroughly amorphous, the journal gave ease and heartiness to my literary dialogue, relieving the solemn and potentially tense interface between "artist" and "art." In a musical sense, keeping the journal completed the harmonics of the author-text dialogue, and in so doing turned an intense two-part interaction into a self-sustaining little world.

With this in mind, it may be helpful to look back at Chapter 3, "The Liberty of Ideas." That chapter treats the literary device known as copia as a way of opening up the mind to the various impulses, emotions and points of view that inhabit it. Journal-keeping, as I have described it here, performs an analogous function in terms of our relationship with the verbal media we employ. Journal-keeping is a mental exercise that keeps us actively involved in language and allows expression on many levels. Liberating and creative in and of itself (each journal is itself an artifact), journal-keeping has the greater virtue of displacing our emotional overloads and allowing us to concentrate more powerfully on the work at hand. It offers as well the precious bonus of putting us in touch with our emotions, which then may be channeled more freely into what we are working on.

All this, however, comes at a price. There is, first off, the brute labor of adding a substantial new activity to one's workload on a daily basis. There is also the difficulty of *learning* to keep a journal. What style should I write in? Must I be grammatical and write as though someone else might someday read it? How intimate ought I to get? There is, last and worst, the pure risk of opening oneself up, of reifying in material terms the weaknesses and excesses one has learned to keep secret, of admitting confusion, of acknowledging fear. No matter how carefully one locks up one's journal after work, no matter, even, if the journal is not on paper at all but rather in a locked computer file to which one's memory alone is key, the mere fact of having put personal concerns into words carries a certain dread and shame: such is the demonic power that an artifact can exert on its creator.

But these woes, awful as they may seem, tend to diminish and drop away with practice. In my own life, the practice of journalkeeping has become part of my work, part of me; I would feel diminished without it. When I was a child I kept a diary out of nostalgia and a fascination with time; as a teenager I used a journal as a confidant; in middle years it is a professional medium. I hope someday to keep a journal for the journal's sake and to turn its attention away from workshop concerns and out into the world.

THOUGHTS ON INVENTION AND DIALOGUE

I will often intensify my dialogic relationship with a text I am writing by not looking at a given chapter for a few weeks after writing the rough draft. Thus, when I come back to it, the text has a strangeness that facilitates reappraisal and revision.

⁊   Perhaps the greatest value of journal-keeping for a writer is the simple fact that *journal-keeping is writing:* that as such, the practice reminds writers of who they are and what they are doing, keeps them engaged in their pursuit, keeps them in touch with their feelings. I have called the journal a lounge, a locker room and a studio; now it seems like a kind of hallway, between our dark reticent privacy and the brightness of expressive endeavor.

ᴄ﹙ᴐ Earlier in this chapter I wrote that via journal-writing I created a mental landscape for my novel, even though I had not yet begun writing it. This metaphor may be extended to later phases in the process of composition, particularly with longer works. A half-finished book manuscript exists not only as a physical artifact but as part of a landscape or matrix in its writer's mind. This landscape or matrix includes the ramifying potentialities of what has not yet been written, the conscious and unconscious associations of what has been written, the physical conditions of writing, the emotional tone generated by the writing process and the personal events (actual and/or emotional) that gave rise to the project. Each time an author sits down to write — and other times as well — he or she should go back into this environment, wander through it, explore it, probe its mysteries. As often as not it will yield more hints for the future than are available through the conscious choice-making of professional strategy.

ᴄ﹙ᴐ Niccolò Machiavelli once wrote to a friend that as he sat reading ancient authors, he would ask these authors questions and they would answer him (see Chapter 8). What he seems to have meant is that subtly written texts *do* raise questions in the reader's mind, and that the reader's subtle interpretation of these questions, if it approximates the author's implicit intention, constitutes the author's answer. We may infer something similar about the author-text dialogue. Both questions and answers about a developing text can be found in the text itself and in the mental landscape that has generated around it.

ᴄ﹙ᴐ I once shared my enthusiasm for journal-keeping with Lee Minoff, a writer and psychoanalyst who has a serious interest in the creative process. When I told him that journal-keeping added a third voice to the dialogue between writer and text, he answered, "Yes, and a fourth voice, too — a voice from within." What Minoff meant was that a full dialogue between author and text, a dialogue that is open and intimate, liberates impulses and images that otherwise would have remained locked up beneath consciousness. This freeing-up allows not just for four but for many voices: for a copious interplay of tonalities and perspectives.

ॐ The dialogue with one's text is in a special way a dialogue with oneself. Imagine the light coming from your eye to a mirror, which reflects the eye's image back upon itself. In the dialogue of invention, the text is analogous to the mirror, but a mirror whose complex living medium distorts us, narrows us, stretches us, shocks us with its newness. If my relationship with a text is dynamic enough, I am rewritten by what I write.

ॐ In Chapter 3 I discussed copia, a rhetorical tool that was suddenly redefined as a source of philosophical insight. In this chapter I have discussed texts and journals that, in effect, speak back to us as we are writing them. From these two examples I derive the following premise: *humanity is in constant dialogue with its own tools and artifacts.* Our products, as discrete, self-contained entities, are fertile in new uses, new purposes. The Old Testament is reappropriated by Christianity, becoming in a sense a new text. Saint Paul takes the sword of Rome and turns it into a symbol of faith. Marx bends Hegel's dialectic to the purposes of materialism; the feminists take Marx's class consciousness and transform it into gender consciousness. Gunpowder, invented in China for firecrackers, is adopted by the West as a lethal weapon, while gadgets invented for destruction are routinely converted into private-sector safety devices and scientific instruments. However inanimate they may seem to be, our productions do not sit silent; they talk to us, and we must answer them. To ignore this is to be insensitive both to progress and to danger.

⌘ I finished the first draft of these meditations on November 18, 1992, in the study of our rented house in Berkeley, recording the work in my journal as follows:

> Wonderful day yesterday: took Ted to school (on way boarded city bus to give Nick his forgotten lunch), then wrote new preface, then rested on my bed in the sunlight, then drove to campus, had pizza & coke at Bear's Lair, worked hard on anthology for 90 minutes, then picked up Ted, shopped, biked alone in Inspiration Point. Except today I woke up sick. I think I'll just futz around today, adjusting. The sample is just about ready to be read.
>
> 1:46. Instead I'm working on Invention.

Now, on March 6, 1994, brilliant Sunday, one day shy of my son Nick's fifteenth birthday, I sit in my office in Eugene, having come, in the course of revising this chapter, into the same room of this literary house again. It has an almost wholly different feel for me from what it had sixteen months ago. Then I was caught up in the first stages of composition; the idea was drawing me forward with such power and excitement that I had little chance to pause and take stock. Now the book is no longer my master/mistress; it is more like my child: my child, who has come home rather scuffed and bruised after tussles with less-than-enchanted publishers; my child, who can fill me at very short notice with delight or terror; my child, who wants affection and grooming and fattening up. Such familiar and proprietary feelings motivate me, but I must limit them if I want the book to develop in its full vigor and strangeness. If I make the book too smooth, it will be smug. And revision, no less than composition, affords the opportunity of listening for ideas that are completely new.

FOURTH INTERLUDE

Backgrounds and
Reflections

I suggested in the Introduction that the primary issue addressed by dialogic thought was subjectivity: the mind's entrapment in a limited and fixed perspective. This issue is nothing new; on the contrary, it has been with us since early literature and is one of the most explicit topics of modern thought. Mooted by Darwinists, Marxists, Freudians, physicists, feminists and other critics of awareness, the problem has become so fixed in contemporary discourse that it has entered common speech ("mindset," "paradigm," "ideology," "attitude") and is now standard fare with schoolteachers, social workers and management consultants, while literary theorists confront subjectivity with the concept of "alterity" or "otherness."[31]

Specifically dialogic responses to subjectivity have not been wanting either. I have already mentioned Martin Buber and Hans-Georg Gadamer. Buber sees meditative dialogue as a radical self-transcendence, a brilliant revelation of the world and God. He is particularly compelling in his emphasis on multiple meditative modes, which have a coincidental resemblance to forms of

---

31. See note 1.

Renaissance *copia*. He is, along with Alfred North Whitehead, preeminent among modern philosophers in his understanding of everyday experience as the theater of true vision, and his attitude toward the everyday is unforgettably poetic and intuitive. But his religiosity is so consuming, indeed so romantic, that it overpowers his other insights. Like the youthful Plato, he builds a handsome ladder and then, in a passion of untranslatable certainty, throws the ladder away.[32]

Like his teacher Martin Heidegger, Hans-Georg Gadamer sees the philosophical quest as a loop in which the observer opens up an understanding of the observed through constant rereadings and reconstructions of self and subject; more generally, he views experience as a kind of ballgame between observer and observed, in which each play or stroke opens up a new vision of what has gone before. Gadamer's expertise in ancient Greek philosophy, combined with his thorough conversance with modern philosophical thought, gives his work a unique sophistication, though it is at times unclear whether he is genuinely internalizing vari-

---

32. See Buber, "Dialogue," in *Between Man and Man,* and *I and Thou;* Bergman, *Dialogical Philosophy from Kierkegaard to Buber;* Friedman, *Martin Buber: The Life of Dialogue.* Friedman's introduction to Buber's *Between Man and Man* and Buber's afterword to the same book are helpful as overviews. Buber's work has much in common with the thought of Franz Rozenzweig and Eugen Rosenstock-Huessy and exerted an influence on Karl Jaspers, Albert Camus and Emmanuel Levinas, among others. On Plato, see Chapter 11.

Alfred North Whitehead was a British philosopher who spent the last two decades of his career at Harvard University. His life and work are testaments to the belief (first voiced by the ancient Greeks) that philosophy is a universal mode of inquiry, not to be bounded by specialties or departments. See, for example, his *The Aims of Education* and *Adventures of Ideas;* also Felix Frankfurter's prefatory essay, "Alfred North Whitehead," in the Mentor paperback edition of *The Aims of Education.* On the narrowness of academic philosophy, see Whitehead's *Process and Reality,* pp. 337–42. Two other excursions from philosophy into daily life have been attempted by scholars who have lectured at Harvard: Richard Wollheim's *The Thread of Life* and Robert Nozick's *The Examined Life.*

ous thought systems or simply negotiating his way among them. His ultimate limitation, however, is that, unlike Buber's, his notion of dialogue never carries him beyond academic discourse and into the world of human interaction. In a manner typical of his profession, Gadamer has devoted his life to other writers and the issues they raise while the book of life lies unopened before him.[33]

Analogous forms of thinking abound in the creative and interpretive arts, the social sciences and many other disciplines. Mikhail Bakhtin applies dialogics to the interpretation of prose narrative, while Carl Jung sees dialogue as an avenue to psychological liberation. Werner Heisenberg and J. Robert Oppenheimer have explored the dialogic implications of modern physics.[34] In our most recently developing mode of discourse, computer language, we have hypertext (a means of moving dialogically from one level of text to another) and interactive media (programs that actually respond to the user's initiatives).[35]

---

33. On the dialogic process known as the "circle" or "loop," see Gadamer, *Truth and Method*, pp. 235–40 (II.1.A.i), itself an interpretation of Heidegger's *Being and Time*, p. 195 (I.5.32; German edition p. 153). For the game metaphor, see *Truth and Method*, Supplement II, pp. 491–98. Gadamer mentions Buber briefly in his autobiographical *Philosophical Apprenticeships*, pp. 154–55, 171, but not as a dialogic philosopher. An interesting parallel to the argument of Gadamer's "Supplement" appears in Hannah Arendt's *The Life of the Mind*, Vol. 1 *(Thinking)*, pp. 179–93. Neither Buber nor Arendt cites Gadamer on this topic, though Buber writes critically of Heidegger in *Between Man and Man*. My critical view of Gadamer's attitude toward philosophy and life is supported by his own statements in *Philosophical Apprenticeships*, where he characterizes himself as a political ingenue. This is perhaps an effort to explain his behavior under the Nazi regime, which he neither protested against nor escaped from, remaining a professor at the University of Leipzig throughout World War II. See *Philosophical Apprenticeships*, pp. 93–102.

34. See Heisenberg, *Physics and Philosophy*, and Oppenheimer, *Science and the Common Understanding*, on the subject of "complementarity."

35. The scope of dialogic thinking in current academic discourse is suggested by three collections of essays: *Dialogue: An Interdisciplinary Approach*, ed. Marcelo

How much of this thinking is truly dialogic? Speaking loosely, all of it. But if we were to define "dialogic" more stringently, as thinking that encompasses not only diverse viewpoints but also (in the manner of copia) diverse disciplines and that gives ear to emotion as well as to logic, then there are few dialogic thinkers indeed.

In the chapters that follow I refer to various of the authors and methods cited above where appropriate, and a bibliography is included at the end of the book. But I must warn the reader that my goal is not inclusiveness and that I feel no obligation to criticize or evaluate all of the writers whom I quote. My process is topic-driven rather than author-driven, and I aim for engagement with a given issue rather than coverage of all its aspects.

A further word about interludes. I have seen interlude sections in books before, but only in textbooks, where the author is trying to add variety to the reader's experience or suggesting that the book's subject matter operates on more than one level. I have the same reasons for writing interludes, but also a third: doing them challenges and expands my own awareness, suggesting new connections and directing me into areas that I otherwise might ignore. For similar reasons, I have allowed some chapters to dissipate into disconnected paragraphs rather than end the way chapters normally do. This may be sloppy, and it's definitely not the way we are taught to write by professors and editors. Essays and chapters, they tell us, should be coherent and inclusive; they should follow through.

Some subjects, however, do not always admit of inclusive and

Dascal; *The Interpretation of Dialogue,* ed. Tullio Maranao; and *The Dynamics of Dialogue,* ed. Ivana Markovà and Klaus Foppa. Of these, the first is by philosophers and linguists, the third by sociologists and psychologists. The Maranao is the most truly interdisciplinary of the three and holds the most general interest for readers. Also helpful is David Bohm's pamphlet "On Dialogue," available from David Bohm Seminars, P. O. Box 1452, Ojai, CA 93023.

coherent treatments. They are what you might call shaggy subjects: topics so full of contradictions and ramifications that it
would be barbaric and unfair to package them in essayistic treatments. Free thought and dialogue are among such subjects. In
writing of these forces informally, disconnectedly, in interludes
and meditations, I try not only to describe them accurately but to
demonstrate them at work.

PART TWO

FREEDOM AND DIALOGUE

IN SOCIETY

5

Social Channels of Free Thought

Large institutions, from nations down to schools and corporations, have communicative systems analogous to the nervous systems of animals. These systems comprise all communicative modes, including the doors, windows and hallways of the architecture, the relationship between floors of a building, the interrelationship of buildings or branches, the vocabulary and structure of professional language (including computer software), the electrical and electronic hardware, the memos and newsletters and data resources, the amount of time available for communication and the overall communicative strategy or tradition.

Obviously, some systems are more open than others; compare, for example, the CIA and the *Washington Post*. The comparative openness of a system depends on its size and resources, its history and its sense of its own purpose. But equally obviously, systems where communicative flow is impeded are less amenable to dialogic interactions, innovation and organic growth than open systems. In an impeded system — a police department, an army, a church-run school — change will come largely from the top, while in an open system — a scientific academy, a retreat, a think tank, a corporate team — change may originate anywhere. Because innovation and growth are recognized as necessary, the openness of a system is seen, or ought to be seen, as an evolutionary plus. In an open system you have, instead of only a few, hundreds or thousands of eyes and ears to warn of danger or report opportunity. In an open system every employee is in touch with the affairs of the institution and feels responsible for its well-being.

But openness is limited by security. Intelligence organizations withhold information that might endanger the lives of their operatives and information relating to their own secret information-gathering. Generals and admirals withhold information about strategic decisions until the strategies can be put in place. Analogous though less dramatic circumstances obtain in business. Corporate executives discuss possible plant closures and layoffs in secret; new model plans are kept under wraps. Secrecy protects the corporation from the outrage of endangered employees and from the depredations of competitors. And corporations are not alone in this. Security of some sort is a factor in any institution whose employees are affected by the strategies of its leaders.

It follows that the freedom or evolutionary capacity of an institution depends to a large extent on how fully it can reconcile openness with security — that is to say, how it can maximize openness without dangerously weakening security. In small, growing institutions this often is not a problem. Suppose that we, a group of four executives and twenty commission-seeking salespeople, were marketing Webster, a recently patented robotic handyman. There would be no market to protect, as the robotic handyman market is not yet in existence. By the same token, there would be no competition. Because of this, and because our interests as executives and employees would be almost identical, there would be no reason to withhold information and suggestions from one another and every reason to share information and test new ideas. Because we are on a frontier, we think and converse like pioneers: we are innovative, frank, sharing.

But suppose, a few years down the line, a work force of 1800, a market share of $2 billion a year, and competing robotic handyman manufacturers in Korea and the Netherlands. Would we discuss Willie, our still-under-design next model line, with our sales force and dealers? Would we let them know of our discussions about moving the plant to Mexico?

The openness/security balance, however, is not a factor of political and economic necessity alone. Institutional psychology often figures in it, unnecessarily tilting the balance and cutting off avenues of communication. Let me give a few examples.

I. COLD WAR SCIENCE, TOKYO COMMUTER TRAINS

In the fall of 1992, a group of scientists engaged in developing nuclear fusion technologies lodged a protest against the United States government. Federal restrictions on classified information, they said, were curtailing their work on crucial projects by not allowing them to communicate with one another. After months of consideration, the government relented and declassified the information in question.

A classic confrontation between two systems: On the one hand, the government is intent on protecting fusion technology because of military considerations. This policy is based on cold war conditions in place since the USSR developed a fusion (hydrogen) bomb in the 1950s. Why didn't the government ease restrictions after the de facto conclusion of the cold war in 1991? Probably because government bureaucracies instinctively want to protect anything that seems to them potentially dangerous. Bureaucracies, characteristically intent on security, are secretive and suspicious.

On the other side of the question, we have possibly the most open system in the world, modern science. Utopian in its communicative philosophy, natural science thrives on the immediate publication, universal distribution and frank discussion of findings (see Chapter 10). Scientists have long known that given their professional goals, personal success is more readily available through openness and sharing than through secrecy and hoarding. They have given shape to this philosophy with a plethora of journals and meetings. They are so keen on inquiry and disclosure that they are apt to offer open airings even to truly dangerous subjects (e.g., genetic engineering today, nuclear power in the 1930s).

The energies of modern science are so great, and its potentialities so multifarious, that oversight from other social sectors is sometimes in order. But if these other sectors are hampered by unnecessarily cautious institutional attitudes, science is robbed of its greatest strength.

Deprivation at once more radical and more universal occurs when an entire culture is systemically denied critical information. This denial, characteristic of oppressive regimes, is all the more dramatic when it occurs in nations self-proclaimed to be free. I quote a recent article in the *New York Times*:

> TOKYO, May 14 [1994] — The residents of the pleasant middle-class neighborhood of Kyodo never imagined themselves as firebrands. But when they heard that the government planned to improve the old commuter rail line crossing the area's narrow streets with a multibillion-dollar elevated railway, they did something extraordinary: They demanded to know why.
>
> Traditionally, the government bureaucracy has made such judgments in secret, and the people simply have had to endure them, with few means of taking part in the process or shaping the outcome. But faced with the destruction of their neighborhood's quiet charm, a group of Kyodo residents wanted to know why this plan had been chosen over less disruptive alternatives, like tunneling.[36]

---

36. "Japanese Begin to Crack a Wall of Official Secrecy," *New York Times,* May 15, 1994, p. A1.

When their government refused to allow them access to its decision-making process, Japanese citizens sued and won. In so doing they not only availed themselves of information vital to their own lives but also challenged a system of guarded information that had prevailed in Japan for centuries. In spite of Japan's parliamentary and elective reforms, this closed informational policy had maintained the old imperial spirit of centralized authority, with its necessarily deep effects on culture. Thus the Kyodo insurrection can be seen as a victory for democracy: a step in driving home the communicative implications of popular government.

Obviously, such revolutions diminish the immediate security of government: its efficiency and autonomy in decision-making. Obviously, citizens armed with vital information might exploit it ignorantly and chaotically. But free institutions, with their immediate vitality, their multitude of possibilities and their sensitivity to danger and change, would seem to justify this tradeoff.

2. VERTICAL MANAGEMENT

The modern corporation is a basically vertical structure (resembling, as has often been noted, an inverted tree) with many levels of authority, each level having substantial power over the next one down. Look at the flow of information in a system of this sort. In general, information — ideas, initiatives, news reports, etc. — obeys what you might call data gravity, emanating at the top and flowing down. All too often, this flow is impeded by the upper echelons, who for self-protective reasons do not want the rank and file to know too much about what is going on and especially about what is being planned. Thus, lower echelons often suffer from a data famine and can only speculate on the priorities and alternatives driving corporate policy. Moreover, initiatives originating on lower levels face numerous stages of possible negation and seldom reach decision-making levels without having been quashed, mislaid, co-opted or committeefied. Lower-echelon people who try to end-run their ideas to the policy-making level routinely run into — how shall I say? — data bodyguards, who screen out information and write polite letters of rejection or deferral on presidential stationery.

If you wanted to find a physiological metaphor for this structure of ideas, you might best describe an animal that can move its own body and limbs but not feel them — a brain in control of its body but out of touch with it. Such a structure rejects its own vitality and stifles its own growth.

3. MONEY CHANNELS IN PUBLISHING

In 1982, at a lunch celebrating the publication of my first trade book, a publishing executive asked me an apparently harmless question: "Where in a bookstore would you display this book for sale?" I could not answer. In the four years since I had started writing the book, I had not given that question a moment's thought. But hidden in it was a powerful truth about marketing, the truth that money, like water, flows in channels, and that projects that ignore these channels are likely to come up dry.

Not that I hadn't had channels enough to choose from: travel, spirituality, psychology, sports, medicine, wellness, fitness, healing, food, memoirs, essays, philosophy, history, humor, science, nature, technology, education and a slew of other nonfiction categories, not to mention poetry and a few dozen fictional genres, all rivulets in the money delta, all sources of known custom and steady income. Their formal separation from each other on bookstore shelves is only part of the fragmenting effect they have on literate culture. They are separated from one another in bibliographies, catalogues, libraries and literature courses. They are distinguished in marketing and market research. They suggest discrete elements and experiences in readers' minds ("I could use a good thriller"; "Let's buy Dad a travel book!"). They influence reviewers in their choice of what to review. Finally, and perhaps most important, they generally determine what sort of manuscripts publishers will accept and so become avenues down which authors necessarily exert their creative energies. These market channels give the American book industry, and hence current American literature, their overall shape. They largely dictate what will be written and read and what will not.

This delta of market channels is another example of what I have described repeatedly in earlier chapters: a system of discourse or interpretation that is limited by the very infrastructure that gives it stability and power. What do publishers lose when they limit their purview to market channels? They lose, among other things, the future: countless unconventional ideas and treatments that might enrich and renew the world of discourse.

Here, as with the cold war science example above, considerations of security rob a communicative system of openness and impede the flow of ideas. But here, dramatically, the culprit is not a jittery federal bureaucracy; rather, it is a free industry choosing the security of established markets over the risks inherent in an open system. Here, in other words, a free system is choosing not to be free.

4. DEMISE OF ELOQUENCE

Let us return briefly to the democratic balance between freedom and equality that I discussed in the Introduction. The relative nature of social equality and its perpetual endangerment by competition necessitate free speech, for free speech is a kind of watchdog against emergent inequalities. Free expression is the first freedom to be guaranteed, the last to be surrendered; but free expression is all but useless without the power of eloquence. By this I mean that discourse of liberty must be lucid and incisive, and it must focus on all matters of moral or social importance. Eloquence humanizes liberty, fulfills it, communicates it for others to use. Eloquence explores the issues of debate that are inevitable in free society and ensures that they will be argued civilly. From the perspective of this chapter, eloquence is one of the key channels of free thought — a direct avenue from the frontier of ethical and political inquiry to a literate reading public. But during the twentieth century this avenue has been severely narrowed by the alienation of intellectuals from the middle and ruling classes.

Take the United States as an example. The freethinking tradition in American letters from *The Federalist* (1787–1788) to Mark Twain (d. 1910) created a forum of discourse in which the cutting edge of social theory, expressed in clear conversational English, was immediately available to a large reading audience. Ralph Waldo Emerson and Henry David Thoreau, both innovative and profoundly influential thinkers, expressed themselves in limpid prose and were subjects of lively conversation and debate among contemporaries from many disciplines. Thoreau's *Walden* had more than ninety reviews, many in local newspapers. The trend-setting novels of Hawthorne and Melville, the revolutionary poetry of Walt Whitman, emerged to a readership spanning a large segment of the public. Creative expression and eloquence, the sinews of liberty in practice, circulated freely in a dynamic and literate culture.

All of that changed with the onset of the modern era, and indeed the change I am about to describe helped define the era as modern. In an increasingly technological and specialized society, humane literacy gave way to professional jargon, while "straight talk" and slang took the place of eloquence in oratory.[37] The cultural dominance of the huge city created an epochal rift in the creative arts (including design and architecture) and the world of letters. In letters the two sides of this rift could be described as a mass market serviced by popularizers and formulaic storytellers and a much smaller elitist market serviced by belletrists. The rift

---

37. See Cmiel, *Democratic Eloquence,* particularly Chapters 1 and 5.

Top: Figure 1. William Gladstone
Bottom: Figure 2. Mrs. Gladstone

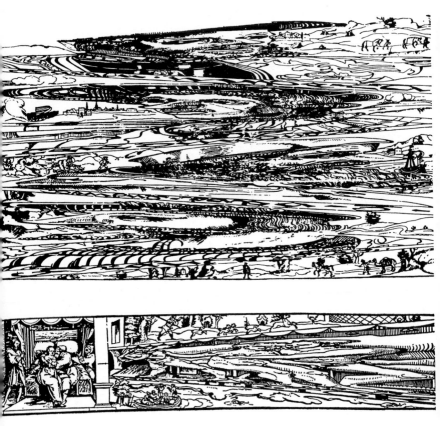

Top: Figure 3. Schön: *Portrait/Landscape*
Bottom: Figure 4. Schön: *Aus, du alter Tor*

Top: Figure 5. Brueghel: *Children's Games*
Bottom: Figure 6. Brueghel: *The Blue Cloak*

Figure 7.
Arcimboldo:
Vertumnus

❧

Figure 8.
Arcimboldo:
Fire

has persisted up to the present time. The two markets are always at odds, the elitists damning the mass market work as vulgar drivel, the mass market damning the elitist work as cacophonic irrelevance. Both charges have merit. But more alarming than either is the fact that the schism between the two markets has severed the discursive artery that once connected innovative thinking with the bloodstream of culture. American society can no longer refine and renew itself through the direct dialogue of outstanding minds.[38]

The emerging democracies of eastern Europe and Asia look to the West and Japan for example and advice and are offered new products and equipment and seminars in communications, merchandising, marketing and management. But we cannot offer them that which we ourselves have lost: a culture-wide forum of ideas, a shared alertness to the permanent issues of democracy, a vocabulary of freedom.

5. CRADLES OF FREE THOUGHT

Touted as cradles of free thought, fairness and open expression, American universities of the late twentieth century are in fact relatively boring places where expression is systemically limited and unfairness is all but routine. These conditions have been brought about not by conscious manipulation but rather by traditional academic and corporate vectors. Let me discuss a few of these.

The Closed Forum. Open communicative systems are typified by amorphous dialogue: brainstorming and rap sessions, often with no set topic, where ideas can be shared and grievances aired at will. Such openness is not present at any university that I know of.

---

38. On the emergence of the popular/elite rift and its effects on style, see Ortega y Gasset, *The Revolt of the Masses* and *The Dehumanization of Art* (containing the essay of the same name; Benda, *The Betrayal of the Intellectuals;* Carey, *The Intellectuals and the Masses;* and Heskett, "Commerce or Culture."

Meetings at the departmental, college and university level are conducted according to Robert's Rules of Order, an ancient system developed for expediting legislation; these rules bar informal dialogue and unscheduled discussions. Particularly *out of order,* according to Robert's rules, would be the informal airing of any grievance against or criticism of department heads, deans, vice presidents or presidents by students or faculty.

The Silent Press. The American press, long famed for its nosiness and noise, is an almost infallible sign of a nation going to great expense in order to keep its doors and windows open: to inform its people about what matters to them and to allow them to share their ideas with each other. Universities (like most corporations) are devoid of such oversight and communication. University publications (excepting student newspapers) are run on a top-down model not strikingly different from corporate in-house publications or media in a totalitarian regime. There is little open dialogue about policy issues. Employee grievances cannot be discussed in print by individuals and are not discussed at all unless they are codified by legal action. This lack of disclosure allows administrators, within certain limits, to act with impunity in cases involving individual employees.

The Fragmented Community. The American university is intensely departmentalized, while each of its departments is full of diversely specialized professors. Specialization makes it difficult for scholars to discuss the research interests dearest to their hearts anywhere except at distant conferences; specialization also tends to produce academic minds that are uncomfortable in a forum of general issues. Faculty members in one department often have difficulty understanding the values and needs of those in other departments. Departmentalization, moreover (together with the university's larger-scale ramification into schools and colleges), inevitably leads to situations in which employees in one sector are advantaged or disadvantaged in ways not shared, and perhaps not even heard of, by employees in the others.

The Compromised Imagination. Except in the natural sciences, conventions and publications at the university level are notoriously rife with ideological frenzy, private ambition and the dynamics of quid pro quo. Communication in these forums is often so rarefied and jargonized as to be barbaric; at a recent medievalists' convention, a broadly parodic presentation, overstuffed with pedantry, pomposity and pure nonsense, was taken seriously by a large percentage of the audience. Many academic journals, while claiming to be refereed (monitored by independent scholars), are in fact the undisturbed bailiwicks of individuals who can deal out acceptances like favors. Even genuinely refereed journals are often at the mercy of interest groups who will not acknowledge the literacy of a submission unless it is written in their own jargon. Under these circumstances, debate on significant issues is limited, and new ideas seldom emerge. Universities give little or no attention to these injustices, which are accepted by faculty members as being part of a dirty but necessary game.[39]

Some of these ills are special to universities; others are typical of large organizations everywhere. In either case, they suggest that some of our ablest scholars should temporarily set their own topics aside in order to evaluate their structures of communication. Our universities, which, under minimal stress from the outside world, have every reason to be open and intracommunicative, are instead clogged-up systems where information is scanty and dialogue is rare.

๑ How can we address these problems? Let me offer a few absurdly brief but potentially feasible suggestions specific to the sections of this chapter.

---

39. A notable exception is the Modern Language Association's annual publication, *Profession*, conceived as a forum for open debate about issues critical to research and teaching about literature.

I. COLD WAR SCIENCE

- Conduct a thorough outside review of federal policy toward classified information of all kinds.
- Research all the official and unofficial ways in which good ideas and products are being kept out of the United States.

2. VERTICAL MANAGEMENT

- Convert wherever possible to horizontal management structures (sometimes called teams) where information, authority and responsibility are shared and ideas flow freely. The Chrysler Corporation did this with success in the late 1980s and early 1990s, by establishing a team of designers and engineers to create a new sportscar, the Viper.[40]
- Via publications, retreats and improved technology, establish organic communications structures: communicative networks where ideas and information flow freely to and from all sectors.[41]

3. MONEY CHANNELS IN PUBLISHING

- Establish a National Publishing Corporation by taking one percent of the annual income of American trade presses (who

---

40. In *Trust,* Francis Fukuyama dwells at some length on team-management techniques in Germany and writes of a hypothetical "communally oriented" workplace: "Responsibility would be pushed as far down the production hierarchy as possible. Rather than maintaining a rigid hierarchy of job classifications that established firewalls between management and labor, a communally organized factory would deemphasize status distinctions and permit a high degree of career mobility from blue-collar to white-collar occupations. Work would be done by teams in which (as a result of multiple skills) workers could substitute for one another if the need arose" (p. 233). Also see Block, *Stewardship,* pp. 28–30, 159, 169, 174–75, 216. Team management has been the subject of much recent publication; see, for example, Peters, *Liberation Management;* Tjosvold and Tjosvold, *Leading the Team Organization;* and Wellins, Byham and Dixon, *Inside Teams.*

41. For a fresh look at organizational information policy, see Wheatley, *Leadership and the New Science.*

will be credited for this in their taxes). This national publisher's responsibility will be to evaluate submissions solely on the basis of literary merit and social value and without regard for market channels, authors' reputations, fads or mass appeal. The corporation will be constitutionally independent of government influence.

4. THE DEMISE OF ELOQUENCE

- ◆ Restore eloquence and the reading skills required for interpreting eloquence to their old positions of eminence in schools and universities.[42]

5. CRADLES OF FREE THOUGHT

- ◆ Revitalize communications at universities by establishing on-campus publications that encourage genuine dialogue and by suspending parliamentary rules of order in faculty meetings long enough to allow for free and spontaneous expression. Establish informal ongoing faculty meetings via e-mail.
- ◆ Undepartmentalize universities by making key areas — humanities, social science, natural science — into coherent entities. Entwine these entities with one another via interdisciplinary programs.
- ◆ Conduct an ad hoc interdisciplinary review of academic journals and conferences. The goal of this review will be not to censor undesirable voices but rather to bring issues regarding the value and relevance of academic publication into national discourse.

---

42. See Heinrichs, "How Harvard Destroyed Rhetoric."

CONCLUSION: INSTITUTIONS AND
THE SHAPE OF DISCOURSE

Human discourse is influenced by factors so subtle and numerous that detailing them would amount to an inventory of culture itself. Nonetheless, it is evident that the shape of a given institution's communicative channels is largely responsible for the quality and quantity of the discourse that goes on within that institution. The superiority of the open communicative system to the closed is as self-evident as the superiority of freedom to servitude or light to darkness. Open systems expand the intelligence and responsibility of institutions, allowing for the exercise of freedom at the individual and institutional level. We in the United States, who have enjoyed the luxury of political freedom for two centuries, ought now to redress the tyrannies that institutional shortsightedness and insecurity have inflicted on our communicative world. Only by doing so can we enjoy the liberty we seek and protect the fairness we deserve.

POSTSCRIPT: INFORMATION AND LIBERATION

In front of the Art Institute of Chicago on Michigan Avenue, Michael Dalton accosts passersby, asking them for a dollar in return for a copy of *StreetWise* (subtitle: "A non-profit monthly newspaper empowering Chicago's homeless through employment," est. 1992). Accustomed to the soft sell, Dalton is mildly surprised when I approach him with money in hand, eager to see what the latest issue has to offer. I'm not disappointed, for the May 1994 number is full of informative and helpful items. Among these are a feature on subway musicians, an investigative report on Chicago's juvenile justice system and an article about the social goals and effects of Loyola University's women's studies program.

There are regular features, including "Eatswise" (listing decent low-price eateries) and "Kidswise," which focuses on "where it's safe to play in the street." Perhaps most impressive is an article in "Helpwise" by Pierre A. Clark (CEO of Self-Employment Enterprises Leadership Forum), detailing simply but professionally the basic steps by which a homeless person can move toward productive self-employment.

From a dialogic perspective, *StreetWise* is a mixed bag. Its disadvantages are that it does not list employment opportunities (though a program of this sort is in the works as I write) and that it is not distributed widely among the homeless. Its advantages are that it maintains communications between representatives of these people and more prosperous readers, that it produces honest income, that it uniquely speaks to the social concerns of the Chicago homeless, that it allows the homeless to communicate with one another and that it does all these things with clarity and dignity. *StreetWise* is an example of an essentially cost-free information channel whose opening has empowered its constituency and enhanced their self-awareness.

What We Need
to Know

AUGUST 30, 1995. WEDNESDAY

Why is today's date important? Because the subject matter of this paragraph is locked in time, as dated and ephemeral as the computer screen that I look at and the keyboard that I strike. Historically, I stand near the beginning of the information highway, the electronic web of communications that is revolutionizing the exchange of information and creating a completely new space for human paths to meet each other in. About two years ago, when many of us in academe were first online, the sense of newness was downright enebriating, and the experience had all the romance of a frontier. With childlike excitement we contacted each other, across continents or oceans, with messages entitled "Are You There?" or "Voice from the Past." My e-mailbox was full of such messages, as well as chitchat from my brother in Vermont, a form letter from someone at the White House acknowledging my note and telling me that someone else would have to read it (no one ever responded), a piece of fan mail from Massachusetts signed "Bored Undergraduate," a memo on the comparative hotness of hot peppers (this is measured in "Scoville units"), a list of the various ways in which nineteenth-century London publicans adulterated their beer, an environmental emergency warning, seven exuberant notes from my wife on the morning she learned to use e-mail and a wisecrack list from one of our departmental secretaries. There was a wonderful freshness to all this. Finding a new medium of communication was like first love.

This excitement passed, of course. The highway, once so broad and expansive, has already become overcrowded with traffic, some interesting but most quotidian and mundane. Whoops of joy have given way to cavils about free speech, pornography and copyrights. Many of the personal contacts, once so lustrous, have become businesslike and automatic. Generally the thrill of new love has subsided into the complacency of marriage.

But, you will object, not *all* marriages are complacent; some couples retain their mutual magnetism down decades of conjugal life. A similar truth holds in the communicative arts. Some forms of information are always fresh and always charged with energy. We may divide this vital information into two sections: forms of information that people consciously desire, and forms of information that are vital whether people desire them or not.

CONSCIOUSLY DESIRED
- We want to know what will bring us advantage and, conversely, what holds danger for us;
- we want access to sources of pleasure and excitement;
- we want genuine, heart-to-heart communication, with confidentiality, and the ability to form networks with the like-minded or similarly distressed;
- we want to learn and to empower ourselves.

UNDESIRED BUT NECESSARY
- We need to know when we are making mistakes or maintaining self-destructive attitudes or misguiding our young;

- we need to know about emergent forces in history that may necessitate our making some investment or sacrifice;
- we need to know about ourselves and the cultural and psychological forces that influence us;
- we need to review and sometimes to amend the very arts by which we analyze and communicate.

The communications superhighway will enhance our lives to the extent that it gratifies these desires and meets these needs. So far, it has made significant progress in this direction. E-mail has created a new mode of personal communication and thus augmented not only the flow of information but the warmth of dialogue. Network facilities, including shops, newsletters, discussion groups, museums and information resources, have opened up new professional, commercial and social channels. The overall level of social dialogue, and hence of social awareness, has risen; the rate of social evolution has accordingly increased. The screen and keyboard in front of me are accelerators of history.

This increased rate of change will bring inconveniences and dangers, which must be weighed beside its opportunities. Organizationally, the communications highway is a mess, and it will continue to be something of a mess as long as access to it remains cheap and easy. But developing fields are always full of disorder, and indeed our attempts at bringing order to such chaos often generate discovery. The screen and keyboard lack the immediacy of personal communication and can thus be dehumanizing. But they can erase distances in space and time in a way that inspires friendly initiatives and special intimacies. Finally, the highway can become a medium for lies; indeed, it is already full of grossly exaggerated self-advertisements. But the same danger lies in any new dialogic medium, from papyrus to television. And the very openness of the system will militate against large-scale deception.

The primary danger of the communications highway thus lies

neither in its principles of operation nor in its moral perspective. The danger lies rather in the possibility that this dynamic new medium will become a vehicle for corporate interests that see communication solely in terms of potential profit. If such interests dominate, electronic communications will lose their vitality and assume the niveau of magazines, cinema and television.

6

೧ೞೞ

Free Thought and
Authority

The political history of the twentieth century can be summarized
as a dialectic of two waves: the emergence of the totalitarian system as a backlash against the liberalism of the Enlightenment, and
the successful reassertion of Enlightenment standards as a direct
response to totalitarianism. Hitler and Lenin opposed liberalism
for different reasons but with equal stridency. Each substituted for
the liberal idea of the state as living organism a model of the state
as machine, and each based this model on a system of control so
pervasively authoritarian as to warp even the thoughts of its citizens. This chapter explores the effects of communism, by far the
longer-lived of the two systems, and inquires as well into authori-
tarianism as an enduring aspect of Western thinking.

COMMUNIST TYRANNY AND
PROLETARIAN DEPRESSION

Just as the first responsibility of freedom is to ensure the amplest
possible forum for communication and dialogue, the first impulse
of tyranny is to diminish that forum to a narrow, monodirectional

channel of dogma. Until the 1990s in eastern Europe, this stran-
gling of ideas was achieved through arbitrary regulation of the
media, interdiction of messages from abroad, severe limitations on
publishing, restrictions on personal travel and stringent control of
educational methods and materials. Because even repression so
comprehensive as this could not fully stop the flow of ideas, governments took the further step of creating secret police who used
informants to monitor the speech of their fellow citizens and who
also made sure that nationals could not speak freely abroad. Only
when these regimes had bottled up all outlets of human expression
could they be confident of their power.

What is life like under such circumstances? The bitterest dia-
tribes of Western anti-Communists are probably inadequate to
describe it. Westerners can condemn oppression and sympathize
with its victims, but they must struggle to imagine the complex of
shame, depression, frustration, bitterness, boredom and dread that
result from what might be called the political realization of a
paranoid fantasy. To enter the mind of an intellectual in eastern
Europe, they must conjure up a haunting sense of unfulfilled
promise, a consciousness of being unspecifiably diminished, an
anguished feeling that their instinctive desire to learn, to know
and to express is somehow wrong and can be indulged only at the
risk of guilt and punishment. Yet those who feel this pain may be
called the lucky minority; for the majority, the political repression
of free thought breeds simply dullness, a spiritual anesthesia coherent with the deadened society at large. Deprived of both individuality and community, people lose aspiration. Their world shrinks
to the material effects around them. Tyranny's deepest offense is
the reduction of its citizens from people of potential dignity to
creatures of barbaric despair.

The nature of this despair is important to us here because of its
relation to the problem of free thought. Depressed proletarians see
themselves as disinherited and impotent; they associate political

authority ("power") with dishonesty, material wealth and sensual pleasure. Never having been empowered, they feel little responsibility for themselves or others; their ethics is based on potential rewards and punishments rather than on what we would call values. Never having been compelled to analyze information or educated to do so, they lack analytic skills and must fall back on street wisdom when reading a newspaper or confronting a personal challenge. Having little or no vocabulary of ideas, they cannot discourse abstractly or formulate large-scale economic or social issues. Having no concept of human equality or diversity, they retain tribal allegiances and are easily infected with ethnic hatred. Untaught in leadership, they are ready followers, hungry for an authority that will rationalize their impoverishment and condone their lassitude.

I make these points in order to dramatize the challenge facing those who would lead Russia and eastern Europe out of servitude and into freedom. Freedom, as I have tried to show, is not simply a matter of law and authority; rather, it is an art expressing itself through subtle and comprehensive interactions among individuals, groups and institutions. For this reason, institutional freedom — freedom under law — cannot be happily implemented if the minds of citizens are not already fertile for it. The results of such a mismatch are evident as I write in mid-1994. What was Yugoslavia is torn up with a civil war whose ethnic and religious roots stretch back through the modern era and whose violence has few parallels in recent memory; other ethnic conflicts have occurred in Armenia and Georgia. Factions in what was East Germany and Russia are regressing to xenophobia and anti-Semitism. Moscow's economic reforms are hampered by profiteering; a crime wave has filled the void left by Soviet repression. What was the Communist bloc is threatened by pervasive disorders, and the troublemakers are often not Communist diehards but the former victims of the system.

Subtler hangovers of proletarian depression survive as well. The price of vodka, which the Communist regime made widely available as a kind of political depressant, is still controlled by the Russian government. Russian newspapers are in disarray. Russian book publishers, permitted at last to range freely in the world of ideas, ignore humanistic inquiries and political issues, instead flooding the shops with mass-taste entertainments. Indeed, with notable exceptions such as Václav Havel, the discourse of liberty, with its evocative ideas and vivid issues, seems as yet unborn in Russia and its ex-satellites. Leadership and the press that covers it seem riveted on economic issues, without a thought for cultural renewal, while the people at large associate liberty more with blue jeans, automobiles and dachas than with intellectual growth, civic responsibility and the clash of ideas. Liberal Russian leaders are ignoring a human factor that their Communist predecessors knew well and regularly exploited: the inertia of the uneducated. The *komissars* knew that of all the great human passions, the most widespread and least heralded is the passion to be left alone and vegetate.[43]

---

43. Two early readers of the manuscript of this book complained that my view of human nature here is unrealistically bleak and that political oppression, via a kind of Hegelian dynamics, tends to encourage an enraged and brilliant counterforce among the oppressed. I can only reply that while I wish this were so, I cannot find support for it in history. The great revolutions in England, America and France were directed by men who had been born into or achieved social privilege (in other words, not by an oppressed class), and this was also true of the revolutions that toppled the Tarquins and Julius Caesar in Rome and the July 20 plot against Hitler. I have found nothing in Sakharov, Solzhenitsyn or the contemporary Russian poets to suggest that things in the USSR were any different. Czeslaw Milosz' outstanding book on the spiritual effects of Communist oppression, *The Captive Mind,* speaks of such regimes as conducting "an enslavement through consciousness" in which consciousness itself is diminished by state prohibitions against expression: "*What is not expressed does not exist.* Therefore if one forbids men to explore the depths of human nature, one destroys in them the urge to make such explorations; and the depths in themselves slowly become unreal" (pp. 191, 215).

Those who would bring the former Soviet bloc nations into the ranks of productive democracies thus face a heavy challenge: the task of raising culture to the level where it can voluntarily nurture the institutions of free thought. Taking Russia as an example, let me suggest a few reforms that would address this challenge. I do this with little hope that any of them can be implemented, but as a means of illustrating the damage that a long-term centralized autocracy can wreak on a nation.

A PROGRAM FOR LIBERAL RENEWAL IN RUSSIA

First, Russia should overhaul its educational system, from elementary school right up to the professional degrees. Teachers must be reeducated in the discourse of liberty. Young Russians must universally, and from early in life, learn of their inalienable freedoms as individuals and their inescapable responsibilities as citizens. They must learn not only industrial but postindustrial skills, arts that will launch their nation into the twenty-first century. Beyond this, those who are specially motivated — a nascent intelligentsia — should be taught the arts of independent thinking: the analysis of systems, the study of politics, the evaluation of rhetoric, the power of dialogue. These arts, which all arose in the West, should be taught in a Western style, although one hopes without the narrowness and lack of conviction that presently characterize much Western teaching. And Russians cannot revise subject matter and method alone: their very language must be expanded to accommodate the discourse of freedom.

Second, Russia should systematically decentralize, so that its discarded central authority no longer survives subliminally in the demographic authority of a central city. This can be done not by weakening Moscow and St. Petersburg but by strengthening regional centers: establishing comprehensive and fully independent universities in these centers and offering tax incentives to corporations, research facilities, professionals and retailers who settle there. Russia, which under generations of autocracy has been internationally powerful but internally dispirited, must realize that democracies are strong as nations only when their citizens are intellectually enfranchised and their regions economically empowered.

Third, Russia must significantly enlarge and streamline its communicative and dialogic structures. By such structures I mean

- television and radio, where central networks must be co-responsive with regional stations,
- the press, which must learn to practice Western tell-all journalism and investigative reporting,
- book publishing and public libraries, where government investments should finance the translation and availability of major works,
- electronic technology, where massive investments should make possible clear and immediate communication in all regions,
- information, where major networks should be available, via modems or hardwiring, to computer users everywhere,
- professional conventions and journals, where nationwide excellence in all fields should be facilitated by an expanded flow of information, and journals should achieve outreach to other specialties by publishing simplified précis of their articles,
- corporate and institutional newsletters, paper and electronic, ensuring that systemic structures remain democratic and open to new ideas.[44]

---

44. In making such communicative reforms, Russia need not take instruction from nations such as the United States and Japan alone. The Russian scientific community, which obviously had to be competitive during the cold war, already has effective intercommunicative systems and can be used as a model by those in other professions.

The importance of these technical reforms should not be underestimated. Had it not been for radically improved communications, which galvanized world opinion and brought accurate news and liberal discourse into the eastern bloc, Communist tyrannies might still be in place there today. Large groups of people will not know the truth unless we preserve and refine the means for telling it.

AUTHORITY IN LANGUAGE

In the preceding chapter I discussed a number of ways (corporate structure, economic channels, specialization, etc.) in which free thought can be warped or suppressed in an apparently liberal system. Each of these ways can be seen as an assertion of authority (by the U.S. government or some publisher or university or corporation) in encouraging one sort of thinking and discouraging another. Now I wish to draw attention to one more form of authority that can work alternately for and against freedom: the authority that is embedded in language.

When Lenin and Hitler installed their autocratic regimes, they did so in ground that was not altogether unprepared. Lenin's Russia had been an ancient monarchy managed by an enormous bureaucracy; Hitler's Germany, though it had been introduced to liberal institutions, was still governed by a bureaucracy, marked by severe social inequalities and ethnic hatreds and characterized by a reverence for patriarchal and authoritarian forms. More generally, excepting England and Switzerland, we do not have to look further back than the late eighteenth century to find a Europe where freedom of expression was radically curtailed by the combined power of church and state, and where there had been few limitations on the power of government since the fall of the Roman republic in the first century B.C. Authoritarian structures, including the idea of authority itself *(auctoritas)*, were suffused through

Western culture via the dominance of the Roman Empire, the centralized church and the Latin language.

Just as the actions of Europeans were governed by institutions of towering authority, so their minds were dominated by the lettered power of books, whose authors' names — Homer, Aristotle, Cicero, Virgil, Paul, Jerome, Augustine, Gregory — were icons of rule so potent as to command immediate assent. This automatic respect for authority persists in the Western mind even today, posing the constant threat of the rise of new authoritarian systems and contaminating even the most liberal of societies, where titles like "senator" and "CEO" command an awe not unlike that brought forth by the consuls and bishops of old. Some liberal thinkers, like the purveyors of copia described in Chapter 3 and the Transcendentalists Emerson and Thoreau, have fought against this mindset, urging readers to forsake borrowed interpretations and achieve independent insights, but the Western thirst for authority is so great that even *their* names are now used as authoritarian battle cries.

This is not to say that authority is never helpful or necessary, or that it is always an ugly thing. But authority is seldom either just or decorous when it is asserted self-servingly and accepted unconsciously. I wish now to focus on two such misuses: a tendency of some Western writers to usurp authority over their readers by methods that suggest a kind of tyranny, and a tendency of many Western readers to capitulate to textual authority, no matter how fallaciously it is asserted. I cite as an example a thinker who has himself become an authority to Western intellectuals, Michel Foucault.

In Chapter 2 of *The Order of Things: An Archeology of the Human Sciences* (published in France as *Les Mots et les choses* in 1966), Foucault develops an analysis of sixteenth-century European thought. He pauses during a lengthy and heavily documented discussion of the Renaissance philosopher-scientist

Paracelsus (whose interpretation of nature, I should note, involved the meaning of various signs) to make a global pronouncement:

> Let us call the totality of the learning and skills that enable one to make the signs speak and to discover their meaning, hermeneutics; let us call the totality of the learning and skills that enable one to distinguish the location of the signs, to define what constitutes them as signs, and to know how and by what laws they are linked, semiology: the sixteenth century superimposed hermeneutics and semiology in the form of similitude. To search for a meaning is to bring to light a resemblance. To search for a law governing signs is to discover the things that are alike. The grammar of beings is an exegesis of these things. And what the language they speak has to tell us is quite simply what the syntax is that binds them together.[45]

What gives this passage apparent authority? Foucault is applying four rhetorical strategies. First, there is the context of the passage in a chapter riddled with quotations from the sixteenth-century authority, Paracelsus. Second, there is what one might call philological legislation: Foucault is redefining the terms "hermeneutics" and "semiology" to bring them into conformity with his own interpretation of Renaissance signs.[46] In so doing he appropriates these key terms into his own scheme of interpretation, thus regulating the reader's response to them. Third, in using words like

---

45. *The Order of Things,* p. 29. In the original, the passage runs as follows:

Appelons herméneutic l'ensemble des connaissances et des techniques qui permettent de faire parler les signes et de découvrir leur sens; appelons sémiologie l'ensemble des connaissances et des techniques qui permettent de distinguer où sont les signes, de définir ce qui les institue comme signes, de connaître leurs liens et les lois de leur enchaînement: le xvie siècle a superposé sémiologie et herméneutique dans la forme de la similitude. Chercher le sens, c'est mettre au jour ce qui se resemble. Chercher la loi des signes, c'est découvrir les choses qui sont semblables. La grammaire des êtres, c'est leur exégèse. Et le langage qu'ils parlent ne raconte rien d'autre que la syntaxe qui les lie.

46. By "signs" Foucault means the visible signs of a system of resemblances which, according to Paracelsus, characterized all of nature.

"hermeneutics," "semiology," "grammar," "exegesis," "language" and "syntax" to describe Renaissance culture, Foucault draws the reader into a narrowly delimited metaphorical world, a world in which all experience is condensed into purely *linguistic* terms, a world diminished from an independent, living reality to an arbitrary human invention. With this metaphorical weapon, Foucault exerts power over his reader, who is pulled into his verbal net; he also asserts authority over the Renaissance as a period, which is now "exposed" as being limited and mechanistic in its point of view. Fourth, the writing seems deliberately obscure. The definitions of hermeneutics and semiology appear to overlap each other, and the statements that follow these definitions —

> To search for a meaning is to bring to light a resemblance. To search for a law governing signs is to discover the things that are alike. The grammar of beings is an exegesis of these things

— are clipped and discontinuous. This is direction through misdirection, a typical form of academic mind control whose operative idea is that readers are more easily impressed and seduced when they are always kept a bit dazed and confused.

In four ways, then, Foucault is empowering himself over the reader. I say "empowering over" because the verbal power used in the passage is not something that the reader is supposed to share. It is not the openly preferred gift of a writer who aims to edify; it is rather a subtle invasion by a writer who aims to dazzle and convince.

Suspicions raised by such rhetoric are certainly not assuaged by the methodology that it supports. Shortly before the quoted passage, Foucault cites, ostensibly as the work of Paracelsus, five quotations from the Paracelsian disciple Oswald Croll (pp. 26–27). This is no error in scholarship: Foucault has mentioned Croll (Crollius) earlier (p. 20), and he correctly attributes the citations in his notes (p. 45; in the original these are footnotes). Instead, it is probably an effort to enhance the text's authority by ascribing the sayings of the obscure Croll to the celebrated Paracelsus. Even more suspicious is Foucault's treatment of the Paracelsian material as a whole. Though Paracelsus and his followers were important in the history of science, they formed only one of many currents in the sixteenth-century history of ideas. By using Paracelsians and Paracelsians alone to support his thesis about the character of the Renaissance, Foucault is guilty of taking the part for the whole: of privileging a minority of data that conforms to his theory while suppressing a majority that may not. Again, the attitude toward authority here is suspect.

Equally disturbing is Foucault's use of Paracelsus himself. Foucault represents Paracelsus as a philosophical purveyor of "similitude" and "resemblance," a thinker characteristic of a whole age that saw "the order of things" in terms of connections rather than divisions. Yet any reader who spends more than half an hour with Paracelsus will find him an arch-dualist who preached the opposition between the astral and the material and held that the world was driven by dynamic contraries.

> Know that there are two kinds of stars — the heavenly and the earthly, the stars of folly and the stars of wisdom.
>
> Everything that comes from the flesh is animal and follows an animal course; heaven has little influence on it. Only that which comes from the stars is specifically human in us . . .
>
> The remedy should operate in the body like a fire . . . and its effect should be as violent as that of a fire on a pile of wood.[47]

Paracelsian thought thus has an intricate and elegant pattern: it is a web of associations set against a weft of contrarieties. In dismissing Paracelsus simply as a teacher of "resemblance," Foucault diminishes him from a complex and subtle interpreter of nature to a simple-minded enthusiast; via association, he diminishes the six-

---

47. From Jacobi, *Paracelsus: Selected Writings*, pp. 39, 89, 151.

teenth century from an age burgeoning with diverse and often opposed positions to a period of pleasant but empty-headed associations.

These difficulties in method bring up the question of good faith. To what extent is Foucault merely careless, and to what extent is he alert and manipulative? The Croll references and the data-privileging described above suggest a consciously opportunistic attitude toward discourse: devious, arbitrary, pervasively self-indulgent. The misinterpretation of Paracelsus *could* be the result of haste and carelessness, yet it is so gross that even if it were, it would suggest a hearty appetite for philosophical self-aggrandizement: Foucault simply looked for data that suited his hypothesis and ignored everything else. Add to this his diminishment of Paracelsus and the whole Renaissance and you get an unpleasant but coherent picture of intellectual entrepreneurship, an image of a man who takes liberties with the authority of other writers and other ages in order to gain authority for himself.[48]

One would think that a preposterous showing of this sort — the muddy scholarship, the superficial generalizations, the transparent self-interest — would have earned Foucault ignominy among his colleagues and disregard from publishers, but in fact he became a fabulous success, influencing thousands of scholars and gaining a reputation for radical insight and bottomless profundity. How can this have happened? Perhaps the best answer lies in the idea of authority. Foucault was a master at taking charge, at constructing a verbal artifice sensitive to his readers' pressure points, at dazzling, confusing, belaboring them into submission. Conversely, his followers were ravenous for authority. Restless, alienated, endowed with short-order doctorates that left them weak in

---

48. Readers may wonder whether I have chosen an anomalistically faulty passage from Foucault or whether I am attacking one of his weak points while ignoring his strengths. I would reply that I have chosen not only typical Foucault, but vintage Foucault.

critical method and dead to the history of ideas, young scholars found in Foucault an island of stability. He had rewritten the story of civilization; he had discussed *everything;* one half shelf of his books could, and frequently did, replace an entire library. And just as he had gained authority over them, and as they had willingly given authority to him, his very name became an icon of almost Biblical power, an authority that could be used to establish shared priorities, justify initiatives, bludgeon down opposition.

The cycle was now complete. The verbal showman, whose discourse was a means to power, had become a tool for enhancing the power of his followers.

A PROGRAM FOR LIBERAL REFORM IN DISCOURSE

It should be apparent that the two halves of this chapter, apparently disparate, are in fact metaphors for each other. Rampant authority is not confined to totalitarian states but also results from choices made by otherwise free people, who, unprepared for independent thinking, doff the chafing mantle of liberty for the convenience of an idol. Set views, chanted idioms and a comprehensive vocabulary of acceptable terms pile up in a castle of discourse which simultaneously protects its denizens and threatens outsiders.

Earlier in this chapter I suggested a program for liberal reform in Russia. Now let me briefly sketch, in the form of ten precepts, an analogous program for philosophical discourse and those who would practice it.

- Philosophical prose should carry the simplicity, personality and directness of the spoken word. Its subtlety and complexity should lie in its development rather than in its diction.
- Philosophers should conceive of and address a reader who is too worthy to be subjugated and too dear to be deceived.

- Philosophical discourse should clearly state its premises, so that the reader may judge whether they are or are not prejudices.

- Philosophy should be holistic and pluralistic, appreciating the value of opposed perspectives and alternate interpretations, prizing the body as well as the brain, attentive to other arts and crafts, grateful for history, despising no experience or detail that can hold a glimmer of truth.

- By the same token, philosophical discourse should decentralize its authority, to be in multiform communication with the reader rather than to move from a single position.

- Philosophical writing should question the reader, cause the reader to question *it,* make the reader self-questioning, inspire the reader to question nontextual life.

- The philosophical writer should be dialogic, realizing that after each successive sentence the reader will carry more back into the text.

- The philosopher should undermine security, exposing beneath each stable monument an explosive issue.

- Philosophy should aim not for academic authority but rather for heroic teaching; its goal is not certainty but liberation.

- The philosopher is humble before truth and disappears into the text.

EPILOGUE

Much of the above, of course, is wishful thinking. Reforming Russia along the lines that I have suggested would take trillions of rubles and a centralized power far more effective than any of the Communist governments have been. Reforming the authoritarian character of Western thought would be tantamount to a universal religious conversion. Yet honest wishes have their function in discourse, even if that function is only to make trouble.

The Meaning of Surprise

Surprise is a natural element in learning and the liberation of thought. It is a component of the great chapters of growth and aging. We are surprised by gaining new skills, by being thought sexually attractive by others, by falling in love, by growing old. I was surprised the first time I had a long and serious talk with another person, and the first time I spoke to my parents as equals and friends. Life is full of other surprises, some quite terrible, but we tend to learn in special ways from all of them.

From a commonsense perspective, intelligent people are not often surprised, because they learn from the past and so are able to plan and predict their future experience. Yet paradoxically, the best minds are always courting surprise, putting themselves into positions where the very texture of their reality will dissolve and re-form anew. Plato said that wonder was essential to philosophy; Emerson advised his readers to "mount to paradise / By the stairway of surprise."[49]

Surprise in the art of teaching functions in two important ways. First, quite simply, students are surprised when they master a skill

---

49. Plato, *Theaetetus*, 155d; Emerson, "Merlin (I)," p. 107.

that seemed mysterious or impenetrable to them before. To realize for the first time the universality of a geometrical theorem or a chemical reaction is to move, with no apparent time of transition, from a narrower to a wider world. This surprise is one of the closest approximations of pure delight and one of the sweetest gifts of teaching.

The second form of surprise is more complicated and is limited to those forms of teaching that might be called philosophical. It occurs when teachers lift from the eyes of students the veil of their own society's fictions: when idols lose their power, when institutionally endorsed and popularly assumed views are exposed as interest-driven fallacies. The results of such surprises range from quiet bemusement to epochal revolution.[50]

If dialogue is a positive feedback loop in which each participant is incrementally altered by the other's discourse, then surprise is a sudden rush of recognition — sometimes as sharp as the crack of a whip, sometimes as soft as a kiss in a whisper — changing not only all that follows but, by redefinition, all that has gone before. Surprise is, in a sense, the spiritual justification for dialogue and the proof that dialogue is free.

Surprise is also an experience that can be used by a skilled rhetorician for any purpose whatever. Foucault employs words like "grammar," "language" and "syntax" to build a surprising metaphor in which human beings are seen as constructing reality in the same way that they construct language. This metaphor, and the surprise it carries, arguably has great value as one of several equally insightful ways of looking at human experience. But as part of the reductive and imprisoning text in which it appears, it can cause harm rather than good. Beware of surprise in the hands of a trickster.

---

50. For another treatment of teaching and surprise, see my *The Grace of Great Things*, Chapter 14.

7

ɕↄɕↄ

Self and Other

Arguably the most radical form of freedom, deeper in its effects than the political and intellectual freedoms discussed up to now, is liberation from the self: not loss of selfhood but rather a transcendence of the alienation of individuals from one another and from nature that is so common in modern society. Many people have found such transcendence in active involvement with others, particularly the sort of involvement that entails personal sacrifice. For people who daily share the sorrows and joys of their fellows, "self" tends to expand into a generous and communal identity. But another, more philosophical form of self-transcendence is also available, one that takes its cue from the idea of dialogue.

SELF-TRANSCENDENCE VIA IDENTIFICATION

I tend to think copiously about myself, linearly about others; that is, I interpret myself as a full and valid complexity of motives, while I tend to interpret other people's actions within a limited moral grid. Such is the endless friction between self and other.

This meditation brings Chapter 3 of this book, "The Liberty of Ideas," to a rather awkward stop. Copious thinking may be very stimulating, but it is ultimately inadequate unless the copia or abundance is broad enough to bridge the gap between self and other: to allow us compassionate contact with selves and voices other than our own. You might respond that copious thinking is in essence self-transcending, because by giving ear to all our inner voices, we are opening up a kind of universal soul. True enough; but it is quite possible for philosophers, after hours of great-souled and altruistic meditation, to leave their libraries and behave like brutes to those around them. Only when their meditation dwells on daily life will they carry the idea of abundance to its full extent.

How can this happen? Not, it would seem, by seeking to annul or abandon the self. Selfhood is born in our condition and flows through us like air. With almost every thought or action I assert or acknowledge my own organic coherence and my differentiation from what is other. But while I cannot deny my selfhood, I can dilate it. I can project a selfhood, unspecifiably different from mine but equally intense and valid, on people near me, even on authors whom I read and readers to whom I write. In so doing I can give these people dignity in my mind; unwrap my mind from itself; liberate it, if only temporarily, from its imprisonment on the two-dimensional plane of subjectivity. I can open up a dialogue, not necessarily with another real person but with my own unfolding sense of what is other.

Artists, especially novelists and playwrights, do exactly this. To create an effective, realistic character (unless one is merely projecting one's own character into the work of art) is to decenter one's consciousness, relocating it in an imagined person who has values, priorities, instincts, manners different from one's own. In the act of creation, the artist's self disintegrates and expands into strange fictive populations, while theatrical players, learning the roles, force their bodies and emotional energies into unfamiliar shapes. Participation in the work of art is a draining and replenishment of identity.

What are the benefits of this displacement?

First of all, relief! A self, especially a busy middle-aged self like mine, is like a big old truck: noisy, greasy, hard to drive, always needing attention. Leaving this self to invent a fictional character or to imagine someone else's perspective is like taking a holiday from the everyday grind.

Second, moral sophistication. Taking on another person's perspective is the classic challenge in practical ethics and the minimal requirement for rational behavior.

Third, strategic advantage. Understanding outside perspectives allows us to imagine how other people are motivated and thus, via a kind of game theory, how they are likely to behave.

Fourth, philosophical understanding. The mind that can regularly free itself from its own boundaries, that can consider a subject from more than one personal viewpoint, has the ease and athleticism necessary for philosophical inquiry.

Fifth, and last, esthetic satisfaction. Imagining another person's perspective, in all its complexity and ambiguity, is always a creative act and thus carries with it the excitement and satisfaction of practice in an art form.

BUBER'S *I AND THOU*

A related form of self-transcendence is the main theme of Martin Buber's *Ich und Du* ("I and You," or "I and Thou"). For Buber, the Thou is another human being or living presence that can be the object of one's fully absorbed, self-transcendent attention. Buber's fullest example of the recognition of the Thou is a series of thoughts about a tree:

> I contemplate a tree.
> I can accept it as a picture: a rigid pillar in a flood of light, or

splashes of green traversed by the gentleness of the blue silver ground.

I can feel it as movement: the flowing veins around the sturdy thriving core, the sucking of the roots, the breathing of the leaves, the infinite commerce with earth and air — and the growing itself in its darkness.

I can assign it to a species and observe it as an instance, with an eye to its construction and its way of life.

I can overcome its uniqueness and form so rigorously that I recognize it only as an expression of the law — those laws according to which a constant opposition of forces is continually adjusted, or those laws according to which the elements mix and separate.

I can dissolve it into a number, into a pure relation between numbers, and eternalize it.

Throughout all this the tree remains my object and has its place and its time span, its kind and condition.

But it can also happen, if will and grace are joined, that as I contemplate the tree I am drawn into a relation, and the tree ceases to be an It. The power of exclusiveness has seized me.

This does not require me to forego any of the modes of contemplation. There is nothing that I must not see in order to see, and there is no knowledge that I must forget. Rather it is everything, picture and movement, species and instance, law and number included and inseparably fused.[51]

---

51. *I and Thou,* pp. 57–58. In a similar way, the archeologists Henri Frankfort and H. A. Groenwegen Frankfort characterized primitive humanity's relationship to the surrounding world as dialogic: "The fundamental difference between the attitudes of modern and ancient man as regards the surrounding world is this: for modern, scientific man the phenomenal world is primarily an 'It'; for ancient — and also for primitive — man it is a 'Thou' " (*Before Philosophy,* p. 12). Buber traces the I/Thou dialectic back to Wilhelm von Humboldt and Ludwig Feuerbach ("Dialogue," in *Between Man and Man,* p. 27); this essay also contains a reminiscence from childhood that offers insight into Buber's view of communion with the Other, pp. 22–23. For von Humboldt's early use of the dualism, see Marianne Cowan, *Humanist Without Portfolio,* pp. 65, 72, 336–37.

Some philosophy is dry and obscure, some brilliant and convincing. But the best philosophy of all is helpful. What is especially helpful about Buber's discourse here is that he is teaching readers to expand their minds into a subject by conceiving of it from a variety of perspectives. Each new perspective enriches the subject and refreshes the mind. Ultimately, a new idea of "tree" emerges, not as a single association but as a shimmering composite of associations.

All this is much like my own encounter with a tree in Chapter 3. But what for me is a way to understand "not so much . . . how a tree feels as to enter the humanity of the tree, the abundance of things that trees mean to people," is for Buber to participate in "the tree itself." Buber, moreover, makes understanding the tree, as a form of the Thou, a step toward contact with God. In other words, Buber equates self-transcendence ultimately with mystical experience. Like the early Plato or Saint Thomas Aquinas, he is an absolutist for whom the dialogic process is ancillary to the monologic Truth that it seeks.[52]

SELF-TRANSCENDENCE AND MORALITY

To whom is dialogic self-transcendence available or unavailable? The answer may be put axiomatically:

Self-transcendence is impossible for me so long as I fear other people or mistrust my ability to communicate with them.

Self-transcendence is impossible for me so long as I reserve one set of values for myself and keep another for everyone else.

---

52. Aquinas' dialogism is evident in the question-answer structure of the *Summa Theologica*.

To understand these axioms is to see the intimate relationship among psychology, values and the philosophical quest. Anxiety and insecurity lock me up within myself, barring the way into the mysterious world around me, forbidding me both the dignity and the humility of philosophical experience. With equal certainty, the moral double standard blinds me to reality. When I empower myself while restraining others, when I excuse myself while condemning others, when I use different moral vocabularies for myself and for others, I close the dialogic window, losing doubly the means of understanding others and myself. The anxious, the fearful, the opportunistic, the manipulative, can neither practice philosophy nor understand the philosophy they read. Advanced inquiry requires moral preparation.

How, specifically, does this dialogue succeed or fail? Courtship offers an arena that is at once immediate and dramatic. Male and female are drawn together by a variety of instinctive, rational and social vectors; profound mutual understanding seems to them an almost inevitable outcome of the love that grows when they are together. Yet other vectors hold them at arm's length. The very gender differentiation that attracts them to each other simultaneously makes them seem alien and incomprehensible to each other. Their longing awakens fears of vulnerability and loss of control. Their excitement and sense of risk breed anxiety and insecurity. From the very heart of the attraction spring impediments to dialogue that can destroy the relationship or persist through marriage.

All this is aptly illustrated in Henry James' novella *Daisy Miller*. Set on Lake Geneva and in Rome, the story centers on a stiff and feckless aristocrat named Winterbourne and his attraction to the beautiful Daisy Miller, daughter of a nouveau riche family from Schenectady. We see Daisy through Winterbourne's eyes. Wholly unsophisticated, she is direct, impulsive, flirtatious. He is drawn by her sweetness and beauty but unsettled by her free manner, which at once suggests American vulgarity (Winterbourne is Swiss-bred) and unseemly sexual liberation. Their conversations with each other, emotionally charged but intellectually vacuous bits of courtship dialogue —

> "Why you were awfully mean up at Vevey," Daisy said. "You wouldn't do most anything. You wouldn't stay there when I asked you."
>
> "Dearest young lady," cried Winterbourne, with generous passion, "have I come all the way to Rome to be riddled by your silver shafts?"[53]

— do nothing to allay his doubts. Daisy's virtue, or her lack of it, becomes his consuming dilemma. Is she a hussy or, inconceivably, so thoroughgoing an ingenue that she is unaware of the scandals she may cause? He follows her from Vevey to Rome, where, to his chagrin, she persists in a series of embarrassingly public assignations with a gaudy Italian *cavaliere* named Giovanelli. Winterbourne chides and warns her, but she stubbornly asserts her liberty. He finally abandons her after finding her and Giovanelli alone in the moonlit and unhealthy atmosphere of the Roman Coliseum. Immediately, as though stricken by his distrust, she takes ill and dies of "Roman fever" *(perniciosa)*. At her funeral, Winterbourne hears, from Giovanelli himself, that Daisy, all appearances to the contrary, was "the most innocent!"[54]

This revelation of innocence exposes an essentially dialogic dimension of James' novella: a dichotomy between Winterbourne's bourgeois perspective and a free-form "reality" which eludes it. This perspective-reality dialogue, according to Mikhail Bakhtin, is typical of the modern novel, which concerns the stress between reality as actually experienced and reality as subjectively conceived. And in the case of *Daisy Miller,* this dialogue directs our

53. P. 51.
54. P. 92.

attention to another dialogue, at once more specific and profound: the social and psychological dialogue between male and
female. This general dialogue, both in its vitality and in its tragic
failure, can teach us something about the relationship between self
and other.

Winterbourne's conscious motive, indeed obsession, throughout the story is to *understand* Daisy: to progress beyond appearances to her elemental nature. Yet manifold forces implicit in
society and in his own mind block this initiative. The gap between
her untutored American vitality and his snobbish European propriety is a breeding ground for mutual misconceptions. Because
of the gender difference, with its two unique and disconnected
perspectives on the erotic, Winterbourne can neither understand
Daisy's behavior nor communicate his uncertainties effectively.
The courtship ritual, with its attendant anxieties, makes both of
them virtually inarticulate on subjects of critical importance to
their relationship. Winterbourne's male psychology traps him in
a goddess/whore dilemma which totally blinds him to the real
Daisy, not only making him distrust her but also causing him to be
attracted by the same behavior that puts him off. More compre-
hensively, they are immured in a spiritually impoverished genteel
mindset — a mentality built on idleness and lack of economic or
social commitment — whose vocabulary is limited to steamers,
coaches, castles, scenery and a few watered-down terms of endear-
ment. Finally, there is the wall, translucent but as hard and distor-
tive as cheap glass, between self and other. Winterbourne only
thinks that he wants to understand Daisy. Instead he is trying her,
as a marital prospect, in a court built of his own social prejudices, erotic compulsions and psychological insecurities. Despite
her challenges to peek beyond his preconceptions, and even after
her death, he never does so. In the end, the playful and inquisitive
Daisy seems sophisticated alongside Winterbourne's labored de-
liberations and moral provincialism.

Read in this way, James' novella is a negative object lesson in the art of understanding the other. Its theme of courtship is symbolic. In almost every case, the act of personal outreach and understanding, whether it has an erotic object or not, is an act of love, of sacrifice and giving forth. Our goal, if we are to avoid Winterbourne's fate, is to rise beyond the identity provided us by culture, class and sex; it is to bring to consciousness and then purposely put aside the specific agendas, aggressive and defensive, that isolate us as individuals. Conversely, it is to let the idea of another person, on all accessible levels of perception, expand in us like a living thing.

SELF AND NATURE

Buber's passage about the tree suggests that the dialogue between self and other is also played out with the natural world. But this relationship itself is a subject of controversy. Is human consciousness able to participate in nature, or is humanity, by virtue of its unique parameters, inexorably divorced from the natural world? Known as the *nomos/physis* (convention/nature) issue, this debate surfaced in ancient Greece, with the Sophists arguing the case for human alienation from nature while Socrates and Plato (following the Pythagoreans and Parmenides) made the case for continuity.[55] Never resolved, the issue was of little concern to the Romans and became irrelevant under Christianity, whose God provided a matrix of associations generously uniting humanity with all other things created. But the question reemerged in the Renaissance and has been particularly visible in the nineteenth and twentieth centuries, with spokesmen such as Nietzsche, Heidegger, Sartre, Camus and Foucault reviving the Sophistic argument against a back-

---

55. For the Sophist view, see Plato, *Gorgias*, 483; for the Socratic view, see Plato, *Republic,* Book 7, and *Timaeus,* passim.

ground of reductionist natural science and weakening religious faith.[56] Their argument goes roughly as follows:

> *When the West lost God, it lost the central abstract principle that justified human values and unified humanity with nature. When the West discovered (via evolution, chemistry and physics) what nature was really like, it discovered a nature alien to human values and insensitive to them. Thus, it is impossible to base moral values on nature, unless we all want to behave like animals. Thus, it is also impossible, except in very impressionistic and sentimental and hence meaningless terms, to "get in touch" with nature.*

This position has been profoundly influential throughout the twentieth century. It has been used to fortify not only moderate ideologies like liberalism and pragmatism but also radical initiatives like fascism and communism. It has generated a familiar mindset — alienated, nostalgic, "realistic" — among Western intellectuals. But it is an increasingly vulnerable position. What threatens it is the evolution of natural science itself. In the course of its own patient and rigorous proceedings, twentieth-century natural science has discredited the nineteenth-century view of nature as alien and inhuman and substituted an image of nature as rational and coordinate with human feeling and value.

The first major spokesman of this revolution was the chemist Michael Polanyi, who in 1958 affirmed that the rationality of the universe had been restored by Einstein's theory of relativity. A generation later the anthropologist Gregory Bateson expounded a theory of learning and nature that was downright Platonic in its harmonic interconnectedness, while the physicist Karl Friedrich von Weizsäker, discussing the work of the zoologist Konrad Lo-

---

56. For the bases of these views, see Kohák, *The Embers and the Stars,* Chapter 1; Polanyi, *Personal Knowledge,* Chapter 1; and Arendt, *The Human Condition,* Chapter 36.

renz, spoke of Parmenidean and Platonic ideas as being essential components of scientific research into nature. The Gaia hypothesis, now favored by thousands of scientists internationally, posits an ecosphere that is the epitome of rationality, responding to stimuli and provocation with the organic coherence of a living thing. Progress in other fields — mathematics, physics, chemistry, zoology — has given nature a much more human face (the metaphor of course should be reversed), while Darwinism, once a bastion of materialism and reductionism, has refined itself to the point where it recognizes value-laden attitudes like altruism and cooperation as being critical in animal and human evolution.[57]

These scientific events have been paralleled, and frequently intersected, by the rise of environmentalism. More than any scientific development, environmentalism gives evidence that human identity and awareness are inextricably linked with the natural world. Environmentalism not only posits an open channel between humanity and nature but warns that we ignore that channel at global peril. While science unfolds a nature that is rational, environmentalism urges humanity to participate in that rationality. The powerful environmentalist term "sustainability" invites humanity to write a kind of constitution with the natural world, guaranteeing that current human uses will be limited to those that will not diminish nature and postulating future uses in which humanity and nature interact in a positive feedback loop.

Given the time delay common in such interdisciplinary transac-

---

57. Michael Polanyi's views on Einstein appear in *Personal Knowledge,* pp. 9–15. Bateson's view is expressed in *Mind and Nature.* On Gaia, see Lovelock, *Gaia* and *The Ages of Gaia;* also Joseph, *Gaia: The Growth of an Idea.* On chemical morphogenesis, see Prigogine and Stengers, *Order Out of Chaos.* On altruism, see Wilson, *On Human Nature,* Chapter 7. On community and cooperation within ecosystems, see Leopold, *A Sand County Almanac.* Recent approaches to natural rationality include chaos theory and complexity theory (see Gleick, *Chaos;* Waldrop, *Complexity;* and Kauffman, *At Home in the Universe*).

tions, the Weltanschauung implicit in science and environmentalism is likely to have an impact on the nonscientific disciplines by the early twenty-first century. Its effect will be to demystify nature and to reinstate humanity and consciousness in a natural continuity. The mental landscape of Western intellectuals will be much less alienated, much closer to the vision of a mystic and the intuitive confidence of a child. Community and engagement will become intellectual rallying cries, and the European prophets of alienation and absurdity will leave the bookstore shelves to join the Chartists and Prohibitionists in underground library repositories. There will be just as many loonies and dilettantes as ever, but everybody will be happier. The happiness will derive from a sense of *belonging* — of being in touch with a larger order — unprecedented in modern times. Indeed, if I may make one more rash prediction, this sense of belonging, together with its causes and effects, will bring "modern" times to a close, signaling the rise of an era when we are no longer alienated by illusions about our identity from the natural world around us.

THE MASS OTHER: A STUDY IN JUSTIFIED PARANOIA

I have discussed the "other" as a presence other than me, a presence with whom I may attempt to identify. Now in conclusion I must look at a different sort of other, the Mass Other of the city or institution. The Mass Other, of course, is actually a set of others, for cities and institutions are made of many conscious selves. Nevertheless, these selves form a mass to the extent that they become embued with a common set of socially determined attitudes and, if you will, a common ignorance of alternative perspectives. To this extent, the Mass Other becomes an incorporated giant, firm in its tastes and unified in its intentions. To this extent, the Mass Other has identity without soul, dominion without compassion. It has dominion because it is a consolidation of social power; it has no sympathy for others because it has no awareness of itself. It is a monster, a cold smug staring face, the brazen image of a self-protective system.

This image speaks but does not listen. Our relationship to it is completely nondialogic, because its power lies in the denial of dialogue. It harangues us with official discourse but shrinks and vanishes at the threat of response.

The Mass Other is not a recent invention. Plato's famous cave dwellers (*Republic,* Book 7), united both in their abject ignorance and their illusion of wisdom, share its character, and it is illuminated by the Old Testament prophets and the thought of Confucius. The modern metropolis, so huge and so cramped, so destitute of both space and time, has created a mass of individuals at once similar to and alienated from one another. The modern corporation, city-size in population but extending across many states or countries, is centrally controlled and in this way is even more fearsome than the city. Add to this the superhuman and still growing technological empowerment of both city and corporation and one begins to understand the birth of a monster like the Mass Other. Population and power have become so overwhelming, so potentially obliterating, that the mind recurrently embodies them in terms of fear.

The Mass Other has all the trappings of a demon fantasy, but psychiatrists cannot cure us of it, for its causes are quite real. It can be dispelled if we escape from cities and large institutions, or if, as I have suggested in the two previous chapters, we attempt to change their parameters, bringing back into them the dialogue and community that they have lost.

One other alternative remains, horrid at first but potentially most liberating of all. We can commune with the elements of the Mass Other that are within ourselves: flush them out, confront them, force them to own up. I cannot imagine a single person so sophisticated as not to carry at least a few of the compulsive gapings, grinnings, cravings and loathings that derive from locality, institution or class. Nothing is so effective an alarm, or so potent a tonic, as the conscious taste of one's own vulgarity. To face within oneself this faceless monster is a braver and more fulfilling act than to denounce it in others.

✑   Looking in retrospect at the three areas of self-transcendence just discussed — interpersonal, environmental and the so-called Mass Other — I am struck with a paradoxical insight: that each effort to dissolve the walls of self, if successful, results in a new form of self-knowledge. Release from the house of individual identity affords us the startling possibility of looking back on it: of seeing ourselves — as architectonic constructions of action and evasion, pretension and concealment, expression and silence, will and fear — from an ampler perspective. Yet the architecture we survey changes, swells, in the act of self-scrutiny, for the dialogic process of self-inquiry renders the self more generous and heroic.

Stage Fright and
Self-Disclosure

Stage fright is currently one of the most common minor psychological disorders in the United States. I say "minor" in the medical sense only. People do not die of stage fright, nor does it make them kill. It is a phobic response that disappears when the phobic stimulus — some present or impending or even imagined exposure to the public — is removed. Culturally, however, stage fright is a major disorder, major because its prevalence bespeaks a comprehensive malaise, a symbolic fear. What do all those people fear? Each other? I think that the answer is somewhat more complicated. The cause of stage fright is less often the presence of known individuals than the sense of such a Mass Other as that described in the preceding chapter. What we really fear is being exposed not to a group of differentiated individuals but to a *corporate* mass: an audience sharing the same institutional mentality or suggesting the faceless masses of crowded city streets. We fear an audience that is cold in the profoundest sense of the word: a mass of people who do not think as individuals and hence have no regard for our individuality. We fear being dismembered by an angry horde or crushed by a giant who rolls over in his sleep.

Why should these fears so afflict us now? The modern city and its technologies are obvious suspects. Overcrowding makes communication difficult because it breeds shyness, embarrassment, paranoia and the urge for privacy. Technology, by forcing us to talk to phones, mikes, cameras, recorded voices and answering tapes, paradoxically stifles our desire to communicate with a real population and instead makes us negotiate with electronic emissaries. The mass market, with its manipulative language and merciless faddishness, projects through the media a veritable leviathan devoted to self-aggrandizement and enslaved to material uses. The dominance of corporations, with their typical depersonalization, specialization and careerism, tempts us to conceive of a social context profligate in its aggressiveness and impoverished of human identity, sympathy and understanding. Other miscellaneous elements — crowds, noise, crime, substances, violence, even the look of mistrust in a stranger's eyes — all drive us neurotically into ourselves and away from the easy and cathartic orality that obtains in less developed societies. In all these ways we are discouraged from the act of self-disclosure, taught to shun it.

And as stage fright deprives us of the release and fulfillment of self-disclosure, it simultaneously robs us of sympathy. How can we give to others, feel for them or identify with them, when we fear them? The ironic and terrible effect of stage fright — the fear of the Faceless — is that it makes *us* faceless: spiritually frozen, functionally incapable of the uses of humanity. Such is the final victory of the city over the individual; here is the breakdown of community, the end of human intercourse and the substitution of modular and mechanical relationships.

Disabilities as subtle and pandemic as stage fright do not have easy remedies, especially if, as I have claimed, they have their basis in social realities. Drug therapy for stage fright is widely effective but has the typical disadvantages of all awareness-altering medicines. Behavioral therapies have proven to be more effective and satisfying. Two therapeutic avenues are available, the first through psychologists who specialize in treating stage fright, the second through public-speaking organizations. Both treatments begin with an individual's admission that stage fright is a problem and that he or she needs help to solve it. Individuals are then placed in circumstances where, with the support of peers and counselors, they may regularly defy their fear by speaking in public. The cure is effected via a process of controlled and gradual acclimatization.

The behavioral cure for stage fright is a telling example of social dialogics, because it involves the partial reconstitution of an individual's interface with society. In the first place, the admission of disability and commitment to therapy are dialogic acts in which individuals abandon their alienated and defensive positions and accept an intermediate role as patients or recipients in a social interaction. In this new role, the surface tension between them and society is dissolved; a dialogic channel is opened; and it is along this very channel that their ultimate input as leaders and contributors will flow. Unlike psychotherapy, which offers insight through self-inquiry, stage-fright therapy encourages us to desist from self-absorption and reinvent ourselves as social beings.

Stage fright and its remedies suggest the spiritual necessity for dialogue: the extent to which individual identity is validated by participation in social discourse.

8

ৡৣৡ

The Wealth of Human Ways:
Dialogue and Diversity

The word "diversity" has been a key element in the moral and political vocabulary of the 1990s. In biology and environmentalism, diversity has come to designate the multiplicity of living species — you might say the genetic abundance — that ensures the continuity and evolution of healthy life forms into the future. In politics and in education, diversity has emerged, via a wholly different route, as an injunction to encourage and ultimately profit from the variety of ethnic traditions flowing into American culture. Though these two concepts have developed separately, they are deeply interrelated. As Aldo Leopold remarked years ago, "The rich diversity of the world's cultures reflects a corresponding diversity in the wilds that gave them birth."[58] And even in their present diverse forms, the two notions retain one fundamental idea in common: that variety strengthens a system and adapts it for change.[59]

---

58. *A Sand County Almanac,* p. 264. This sentence is from the meditation titled "Wilderness" in the section called "The Upshot."

59. The most eloquent popular book on biodiversity is Edward O. Wilson's *The Diversity of Life.* For general insights into the role of diversity in nature, see particularly Chapters 1 and 15. Also see Ward, *The End of Evolution,* and Thomson, "The Uses of Diversity," in his *The Common But Less Frequent Loon.*

It takes but little thought to appreciate the broad relevance of this idea. Behold, for example, the humble wasp. Over tens of millions of years wasps have evolved in thousands of species, each adapted to its particular habitat and often specializing in a particular form of living prey (there is even a variety known as the Tarantula Hawk). The wasp family has benefited from its "appreciation" of the diversity of insect life, and the benefit is passed on to the environment when wasps pollinate flowers, regulate insect population or die to become food for other animals or for vegetation. Look next at medieval Venice. In an age when most other city-states withheld privileges from aliens, Venice opened its gates to all, allowing people from everywhere to trade and profit in safety and thus giving the modern world its first example of a free market. Without any detriment to its religion or security, Venice thus used diversity to gain financial vitality and a competitive edge over other Italian principalities. Consider, finally, Oracle Systems, a business-software manufacturer based in Redwood City, California. In the 1970s and 1980s, while its competitors wrote software that was specific to a limited number of systems, Oracle produced universally compatible programs, programs that could "listen" and "speak" to a large variety of hardware/software configurations. By gearing for diversity, Oracle became the leader in its field.

These examples imply that systems evolve prosperously if they foster diversity within themselves and respond positively to diversity in their environments.

DIVERSITY AND REDUNDANCY

Connected with diversity is a concept that, after centuries of bad press, has enjoyed a measure of redemption. This concept is redundancy. For some years "redundancy" has been used with relation to systems whose components are backed up by other components which can assume their function. In the best-case scenario, these backup components are never used at all (i.e., are redundant); their value resides in their mere availability.[60] More recently the concept has been picked up by biologists, who, finding redundancies in nature's blueprint, have come to see them as evolutionary strengths. Discussing evolution in his *Eight Little Piggies,* Stephen Jay Gould speaks of redundancy as "profoundly important . . . the ground of creativity in any form." He goes on to treat the history of organs:

> If each organ existed explicitly for a single role, then I suppose that one organ doing more than one thing would be rare, and that two organs doing the same thing would be even rarer. But organs were not designed for anything; they evolved — and evolution is a messy process brimming with redundancy. An organ might be molded by natural selection for advantages in one role, but anything complex has a range of other potential uses by virtue of inherited structure . . . Any vital function restricted to one organ gives a lineage little prospect for long-term evolutionary persistence; redundancy itself should possess an enormous advantage.[61]

According to Gould, redundancy is a bountiful complexity, a *richness of potential* built into natural forms and allowing them to evolve. As such it is cognate with the diversity I described above. Like diversity, redundancy is a principle of variety carrying the potential for productive change.[62]

---

60. The opposite of redundancy is efficiency: doing the most with the least. If certain systems on an airliner are redundant, its thin outer skin, at least, is efficient. Built for lightness, speed and economy, it will neither resist bullets nor endure a crash landing.

61. *Eight Little Piggies,* pp. 177–78.

62. In a radio interview publicizing his book, Gould discussed the possibility that the many "junk" (i.e., apparently useless) molecules in DNA are in fact redundancies that enable genes to evolve.

What has all of this to do with liberty and dialogue? First, diversity and redundancy are functionally similar to the intellectual copia described in Chapter 3: all are liberating principles whose power depends on the acceptance or utilization of variety. Second, both diversity and redundancy are extensions of the idea of dialogue. Cultural diversity at its best is a dialogue of cultures in which interaction with the exotic or "other" instills compassion, sophistication, a sense of alternatives and intellectual curiosity. Biological diversity and redundancy are parts of a reciprocal interaction far more distended in time: the mute but eloquent dialogue of environment and species. In this dialogue, sometimes in the space of a few decades but usually over much longer periods, a species responds to environmental change, simultaneously altering the environment it inhabits. Diversity and redundancy suggest to us that nature, as well as mind and society, behaves dialogically and can be examined as dialogue.

Redundancy is a profoundly important idea with a great variety of possible applications. Oral narrative and casual conversation are full of redundancy; so are religious art and ritual. Economics and politics are redundant with systems and strategies which, though they seem impractical at present, may work elegantly under future circumstances. Cultural diversity itself — the wealth of human ways — exhibits the new law of redundancy when we see one people take up a standard of technical or scholarly excellence when others have let it slip. And the idea can pop up meaningfully in surprising places. The physicist Richard Feynman once remarked that when several solutions to a problem are available and only one is chosen as the most effective, the others should be remembered as possible approaches to new and different problems. Redundancy, in other words, can function bountifully, even in scientific method.

DIVERSITY AS CHANGE AND HISTORY

These reflections on diversity have repeatedly touched on the idea of change, as presenting the environmental challenge that diversified organisms and institutions are especially qualified to respond to. It is time now to consider change itself as a medium of diversity and source of dialogue. If this idea sounds strange at first, it is only because diversity, like so many other subjects, is routinely considered three-dimensionally rather than four-dimensionally. But if we open up the four-dimensional perspective, we see that change is nothing other than diversity in time.

This temporal diversity is vast; its extremes are dramatic. It holds not only our own varieties of culture and experience but countless others in untold richness. But access to this wealth is limited. Up to a certain point we may speak and listen to the past's survivors: older people whose testimony recalls, from a distance of two or three generations, profoundly different times and concerns. But beyond this limit, we cannot call the past directly into our classrooms or meeting halls. Instead we must negotiate with its silent ambassadors: relics, architecture, literature, art. We must examine them with a profound respect for the cultural complexity that produced them, but without the awe or nostalgia that would limit our ability to perceive them and leave us, willy-nilly, exiled in our own time. To the same extent that we must hold conversation with the diversity of present cultures, we must open a dialogue with the past that liberates us from the provinciality of the present.

The disadvantages of temporal isolation and the benefits inherent in chronological diversity are apparent in two images from Italian life. Here is E. R. Chamberlin describing the coronation of Pope Boniface VIII in Rome, in January 1294:

> Outside the palace, a curious ceremony took place, an inverted reflection of the one that had taken place outside the Vatican.

There, Boniface had been seated upon the chair of St. Peter; here, he sat down on an ancient red marble chair, with a pierced seat that bore a strong resemblance to a commode. Originally, the chair had stood in one of the great public baths of the city, but its humble origins had long been forgotten, now that it was, like so much else from the great past, swept into papal ceremony and refurbished. It is probable that its antiquity and beautiful color had led to its being adopted as the throne on which the new Pope took formal possession of the Lateran. But its curious shape gave rise to the belief that the Pope sat down upon it in a gesture of self-abasement from which he was to be raised up by his cardinals. A few years before Boniface's coronation, less pious but even more vivid imaginations had begun to spin the story that the purpose of the throne was to allow a physical examination of the Pope, and thus avoid a repetition of another "Pope Joan." The rumors so thrived that two centuries later there existed a complete pseudoceremony of examination, faithfully recorded by the most credulous chroniclers and historians, to give substantiation to the story of Joan.[63]

The year 1294 was by no means the Dark Ages but rather the era of Aquinas and Dante. But the sophistication of these savants was not shared by the church, which had little interest in its own real history and depended instead on inherited (and thus enshrined) ritual. The beautiful and ancient commode had probably been chosen at some Dark Age time when its acquirers had no idea what it had actually been, and their choice had come down to the late thirteenth century as an article of divine ordination. The disquieting rumors about "physical examination" and "Pope Joan" sprang from a gross distortion of tenth-century Roman history, which, because of the wretched state of papal historiography at that time, was widely accepted as fact.[64]

---

63. Chamberlin, *The Bad Popes*, p. 91.

64. "Pope Joan" had actually been a powerful "senatrix" named Marozia (see Chamberlin, p. 32ff.).

Implicit in Chamberlin's understated account is a depiction of shocking institutional self-parody — of a church that, in disregarding its own past, has lost its spiritual validity and upended all its dignities. Without a distinct past, the church is lost in time, no longer a rooted institution but rather a powerful accumulation of arbitrary symbols and observances. Ignorant of its own past, it cannot know itself.

Within two generations after the coronation of Boniface, Italian humanists were to express radically different attitudes. The humanists invented modern historiography by ripping into the ahistorical perspective of their contemporaries as "barbaric" and urging the systematic study of history.[65] The movement was spearheaded by Francesco Petrarca (Petrarch), who raised the idea of chronological outreach to an extreme pitch by opening up a personal correspondence with writers of the past and readers of the future.[66] The Florentine humanist Niccolò Machiavelli, legendarily tough-minded, nonetheless held imaginary conversations with the past:

> Evenings I return home and enter my study; and at its entrance I take off my everyday clothes, full of mud and dust, and don royal and courtly garments; decorously attired, I enter into the ancient sessions of ancient men. Received amicably by them, I partake of such food as is mine only and for which I was born. There, without shame, I speak with them and ask them about the reason for their actions; and they in their humanity respond to me.[67]

---

65. On the humanists and history, see, for example, Stephens, *The Italian Renaissance,* Chapter 14.

66. These works include a letter to Cicero, a dialogue with Saint Augustine *(The Secret Conflict of My Desires)* and a letter to posterity. See Francesco Petrarca, *Opere* (ed. Giovanni Ponte, Milan: Mursia, 1968), pp. 794–97, 432–597, 885–901.

67. From Machiavelli's letter to Francesco Vettori (December 10, 1513), translation mine, quoted from my article, "Humanism," in the *Encyclopedia Britannica.* For the complete letter, see Gilbert, *The Letters of Machiavelli,* pp. 139–44.

Machiavelli describes the act of reading. By "they . . . respond to me," he implies a kind of literary dialogue in which a reader, changed and galvanized by questions raised in the text, looks back into the text (this time, so to speak, with new eyes) for the answers. The act of reading generates a hermeneutic loop between text and reader, and in this case between past and present, in which communicative barriers fall away and a living relationship is born. The text, the dead author, become responsive presences in the reader's mind. In Buber's language, the text becomes a Thou. Nor was this for Machiavelli a vehicle of nostalgia or self-immersion. Realizing that the past could only truly live in the reader's current and realistic perspective, he built from ancient thought the armature of a revolutionary modernism.

This last consideration is critical in gaining a perspective on the past or in establishing a dialogue with it. We can never fully realize the past, wrap words around it, epitomize it. Because of its human and natural complexity, it was untranslatable even when it existed as present. But we can inhale it, savor its irreconcilable unlikeness, play with its alternative ways of being, sift through its soil carefully in search of our own roots. In so doing we can build from chronological diversity an awareness of change and continuity that can well equip us for the future.

THE POLITICS OF DIVERSITY

At the start of this chapter, I gave examples of three forms of diversity (wasps, Venice, Oracle Systems) that held major benefits for species or systems. I went on to discuss redundancy and history as two interesting extensions of the idea of diversity. All of these are genuinely dialogic interactions: direct and significant feedback that is of evolutionary benefit to at least one party. Obviously, these interactions, and the principle implied by them, have social significance. Not only Venice but Great Britain and in even larger measure the United States of America have won human riches from developing the liberal immigration policies and individual liberties that foster diversity. But the subject of social diversity, like all things political, is full of deception and illusion. In order to chart a course for genuine social diversity, we must first look at some programs that counterfeit it.

In the 1950s and 1960s and 1970s, for example, the Big Three automakers in America each produced huge menus of models, with distinctive styling alterations for each model year but little real improvement in performance, economy, safety or quality. In so doing they produced a kind of diversity that, in sacrificing function to form, did a major disservice to the American consumer, and they ended up losing huge tracts of market ground to their more responsible counterparts in Europe and Asia. Here we have a cosmetic diversity, utilized by an industry that was opportunistic, if not cynical.

Similarly, not all forms of ethnic diversity are equally dialogic. In order to show why, let me suggest that there are several types or models of the *idea* of ethnic diversity, and that while each of them is anchored in social truth, at least four of them are subject to abuse.

Diversity as Tolerance. This is a model based on the sound premise that human beings are equal and deserve to be treated with dignity. This premise is basic in all models of diversity, but here it is extended to the implication, usually drawn by professors safe in their offices, that all forms of personal or group behavior, if they have an ethnic blueprint, are equally acceptable. In order to understand why this extension is not valid, we need only remember that many ethnically trademarked practices (like automatically hating other ethnic groups or exposing female babies or selling one's daughters as wives or slaves) deny the human equality and dignity that are the premises for toleration. Diversity can be genuinely appreciated only in a context of political equality, individual dignity and respect for excellence.

Diversity as Stereotypical Ethnicity. This model is based on the simple and valid perception that a group's ethnicity expresses itself in shared characteristics. This perception causes us, in the presence of an identifiable member of a given ethnic group, to expect certain attitudes and behavior patterns. Based on the soundness of the initial perception, this expectation on our part is understandable. But it is dangerous because it encourages us to diminish "ethnic" people in two ways: we may underestimate the extent of their individuality, and we may assess an ethnic characteristic as a limitation without appreciating its role as a cultural strength. Ethnic stereotyping in movies and on television, which is generally indulged in for laughs and generally condoned because it "fosters diversity," is frequently guilty of this diminishment.

Hyperethnicity. Both attitudes described above foster hyperethnicity, a syndrome in which individuals consciously or unconsciously exaggerate their own cultural inheritance. In this syndrome, ethnicity takes on the role of character armor, allowing people to make arbitrary responses, adopt exaggerated postures, disregard minimal social norms and indulge in political extremism. In so doing they subvert the original function of ethnicity, as a language of social cohesion, into a new role as individual or group self-validation, thus closing themselves off from dialogue. This form of self-stereotyping has little social value. It tends instead to stifle evolution, by establishing individuals or groups as militant islands in the current of change. It ignores the principle that is at the root of and hence even more important than the politics of diversity: the principle of our shared humanity. And it can be used by demagogues to incite all sorts of brutality against outsiders.

Politically Correct Diversity. This is diversity acclaimed or supported as part of a political program that considers little else.

Political correctness is identified not only by this unilateral endorsement of diversity but also by the manner in which it is presented — arbitrary, narrow, authoritarian, puritanical, humorless, guilt-producing: a style that suggests that the enforcers do not care as much about diversity as about enhancing their own power. One might say that political correctness is the right ideas expressed by the wrong people. But, one would have to add, only *some* of the right ideas. If, as I averred in Chapter 1, liberty and equality are complementary principles in American democracy, the politically correct fasten exclusively on equality, producing a political medium that is at once purged of injustice and dead to ideas.

    As an alternative and perhaps antidote to these four models, I suggest a fifth, which might be called *Diversity as Evolution.* This is the only model that allows ethnically diverse individuals to interact with one another on an equal basis. The model is based on the premise that all ethnic heritages are in fact bundles of survival strength: historically validated cultural languages. Not all of these original strengths are equally muscular in urban English-speaking society; peoples have been uprooted from or have emigrated from the environments to which their heritage adapted them. Behavior patterns effective in ethnic in-groups, moreover, may be of little avail to individuals isolated in new settings. But history affirms that the cultural packages of immigrants are full of potential wonders, some quite obvious, some perhaps never to be expressed, some so secret that we will know them only from future surprises. To use a metaphor from biology, you might say that ethnic heritages, as self-sufficient ways of being, may be packed with psychological *redundancies,* which, blossoming sensationally during the process of social adaptation, make immigrant groups capable of evolving into the future. Society is unlikely to benefit from these potentialities unless it gives ear to the new voices, views differences with the interest they deserve, honors people as individuals rather than stereotypes and sees diversity as holding the seeds of future change.[68]

While the first four models respect diversity for what it is, this last model also honors it for what it can become.

NOTES ON DIVERSITY

Just above I stated that ethnic heritages are "bundles of survival strength" and that they, "as self-sufficient ways of being, may be packed with psychological *redundancies*," which can help immigrants evolve. I made this remark as a complete amateur; I cannot imagine a scientific way of elaborating or testing my thesis. But I was spurred into the metaphor by historical examples in which ethnic groups transported into new settings have behaved in surprisingly productive new ways. In ancient and early medieval times, Jews, who sprang from a self-contained and traditionalist culture, participated in the cutting-edge intellectual development of cosmopolitan, Hellenistic Alexandria, and later served as intermediaries between Islamic and Christian culture in Spain. In the twentieth century we see first- and second-generation Chinese Americans, whose cultural background is anything but high-tech, rocketing to the first ranks of international science. Via a kind of reverse immigration, major American software manufacturers have opened plants in the Indian city of Banglador, where native engineers, who perhaps had not heard of a computer ten years ago, are now producing superb software applications. But to me the most striking example of ethnic innovation is jazz, one of the most sophisticated art forms of modern times, developed by the grandchildren of slaves. Obviously there was a cultural propensity for each new form of involvement — otherwise we would not see, in each case, such large numbers of a single ethnic group achieving

---

68. On this subject, see Gates, "Beyond the Culture Wars."

excellence in the same pursuit. What made me use the metaphor of redundancy was that these propensities, which were more or less hidden, fulfilled themselves as the result of new social configurations and emerged as surprises.

ᴄᴢ When I speak of ethnicity as a language, I mean more than a special ethnic vocabulary or even an assortment of words and gestures. I mean a full expressive and reflective instrumentation, including words, gestures, tonalities, songs, dances, images, myths, tales and jokes. Born in orality, resistant at once to literary polish and urban propriety, ethnicity is a profoundly emotive language, a more potent means of opening the gates of feeling than either the elegance of belles-lettres or the correctness of textbook parlance. With a single apt flourish, ethnic language can convey the speaker's state of mind; with almost equal brevity it can express the attitude of a constituency, whether family, village, region, class, ethnic group or nation. Its eloquence can convey the mood of the moment or the way in which its speaker and speaker's forebears — Florentines, Athenians, Muscovites, Dubliners — have felt for generations. Ethnicity thus offers survival strength in three ways: by drawing people together, by suggesting their shared history and by letting them give voice to otherwise pent-up feelings.

ᴄᴢ We can make little progress in understanding the nature of bigotry if we do not understand that although ethnicity is its object, ethnicity is also its source. This insight is hidden if we identify bigotry with oppression. Bigotry and oppression, though they often occur simultaneously, are two different things. Oppression is an activity engaged in by an empowered class; bigotry is a way of thinking, irrespective of class. Bigotry arises when the clannish entente characteristic of ethnicity produces, as if by its own shadow, a social Other whom it diminishes or excludes. Such exclusion is not practiced solely by ruling majorities. Many ethnic minorities, oppressed or not, are certifiably bigoted and would be oppressive if they had the chance to be. Thus the cure for oppression is not empowerment per se; it is enlightenment underwritten by political freedom and equality.

ℰℴ   Diversity is sexy.

ℰℴ   Education should not only foster ethnic diversity but also cherish and promote intellectual diversity. And intellectual diversity — the variety and abundance of ideas — demands intellectual innovation, intellectual entrepreneurship: the mind's ability to move into new areas freely and *sheerly on the basis of their inherent interest,* without regard for precedents or departments or fields. Education currently does not allow for this. Education, which should be the leader, lags far behind such industries as communications, computers and even entertainment in its ability to develop new subjects and become a positive force of change. In particular higher education, which should be the real seedbed for change, is mired down in boilerplate courses and departments whose shopworn nomenclature — "English," "Philosophy," "Political Science" — often conceals hopelessly narrow and isolated pathways of study. Universities should endorse intellectual diversity by rethinking their curricula, departmental structures and research priorities in terms of the relationship between higher education and the developing issues and opportunities of the 1990s and early twenty-first century. To make the best of things while this planning proceeds, talented professors should be "undepartmentalized" in order to follow unique avenues of research and create new courses.

ℰℴ   Social diversity is least tolerated and most dangerous in poor and uneducated societies, where many compete for little. Diversity prospers where affluence meets sophistication. But diversity fares most brilliantly on frontiers, where there are emergent challenges and/or a sense of shared opportunity. Two factors lend to this brilliance. The first is that frontiers are such exciting event sequences that they overshadow human distinctions. The second is that frontiers often defy conventional strategies and provide opportunities for surprising new approaches. Thus frontiers foster communality and provide the alchemy by which strange becomes wonderful.

Dialogue and Diversity
in the University
Core Curriculum

The effectiveness of core requirements for the bachelor's degree in American colleges is a regular topic of debate. Are these requirements too loose and liberal? Do they adequately address ethnic diversity? Do they provide cultural literacy? Ought they to be monitored for correctness? These and other questions, put in books, articles and institutional studies, give the impression that, though troubled by certain thorny issues, American higher education is generally self-aware and self-critical on the subject of undergraduate requirements. I regret that this is not the case at all. Alert as we may be to the political ambiguities of our required studies, we largely ignore their appalling narrowness.

I have little quarrel with the requirements — humanities, social science and natural science — already in place. Rough-hewn and general as they may be, they deal with areas of development — communication, value, social consciousness, logic, method — that are of critical importance to the individual and society. But they fall far short of addressing the common experiences of adults and hence fail to prepare our students for active life.

My reasons for saying this should be apparent to almost anyone who looks up from this page and out into the world. The salient feature of the human environment is that it has been engineered. Whether you are looking at a home, an office or a window frame opening to landscaping, farmlands or a second-growth forest, you are looking at human constructs tailored by machines. Engineering and technology have in large measure created modern history. They have done so, moreover, within a shaping dialogue of commerce, fueled by universal desires for security and profit and buttressed and limited by law. This world of technology and commerce and law — which for short we can call material culture — is routinely derided by intellectuals as mundane and boring; yet viewed distinctly, it is vivid and fascinating, not least because it is the world on which everybody, intellectuals included, depends for survival. To deride this world, to minimize or ignore it, is profoundly dangerous and can only be the fruit of ignorance.

Why dangerous? Isn't the most dramatic aspect of material culture the fact that it is so easy to ignore? Modern office equipment — the user-friendly computer mouse, for example — is engineered for simplicity, allowing us, with relatively few commands, to control complex and powerful electronic networks. Machines more and more take on the lineaments of human discourse and are coherent with the human world. But this is exactly the issue. Machines may well empower us by simultaneously growing more effective and simpler to use, but if in the process we do not also improve our knowledge of their basic principles of operation, we are the more dependent on them and hence are diminished. Our knowledge of material culture must not be limited to screens and keyboards, because if it is, machines and their makers will ultimately predesign our alternatives, delimit the way we live and think.

In other words, we must gain knowledge of material culture not only in order to interact with it but also in order to preserve our independence from it. Ignorance of the material context is tantamount to surrender to it.

A similar claim can be made with regard to the commercial/legal world, the marketplace that is constantly shaping our machines and being shaped by them. Though the American image of a free marketplace, characterized by individualism, creativity and innovation, is compelling, it is far from accurate. In fact our marketplace is a huge and subtle network of corporate and governmental channels carrying particular forms of power and resistant to change. These channels largely determine the kinds of projects that are supported, the kinds of loans that are made, the kinds of people who are hired and promoted; on another level, they specify the kind of information that is published, how it is communicated and in what language; more generally, they assert tremendous influence on popular tastes and even on individual values and aspirations.

If we feel free within these multifarious limitations, it is precisely because they constrict our awareness of possible alternatives. Our freedom, in other words, is an illusion. Real freedom is available only through a knowledge of the marketplace and its limitations. This knowledge is thus precious to our commercial, political and spiritual independence. Conversely, ignorance is the demeaning and dangerous acceptance of a narrowed life.

Yet such stultifying and self-endangering ignorance is the normal consequence of an American college education. Most American college graduates are about as analytically aware of engineering, commerce and law as they were when they graduated from the womb. In fact, because of influences generated by their specialized departments and professors, they are probably the worse for their education. Babies pick up objects, explore them, play with them. College graduates take the engineered and commerce-driven world for granted or fear it as an alien force. Any conversance they are to achieve with it will be through professional school or hard knocks.

How did this educational disenfranchisement come about? The

original humanistic concept of education as all-encompassing or "pansophic" had its last major outing with John Amos Comenius (1592–1670). Law, business and engineering developed as discrete professional disciplines in schools occupying separate tracts of university real estate. Colleges "of arts and sciences," thus isolated from the real social movers and shakers, nonetheless bore the responsibility for a liberal four-year bachelor's education. They did the best they could to meet this challenge, developing core requirements that drew powerfully from their own general areas of expertise. But they did not and could not do enough, and their failure has grown more dangerous as material culture has grown in power and complexity.

How can we redeem such deprivation? I suggest changes on two levels.

Administratively, universities should reintegrate schools of business, engineering, law and other professional schools with their colleges of arts and sciences. This can be achieved in a number of ways, but what is essential is that each profession develop a series of general undergraduate course offerings that are accepted as essential elements of liberal studies. Moreover, via programs, colloquia, grants and released time, a dialogue between the long-alienated disciplines should be initiated. This dialogue should redress such truly shocking divisions as those that currently exist between law and ethics, law and political science, business and economics, engineering and architecture, communications and psychology; it should be aimed at establishing an integrated view of the disciplines and their social roles.

Pedagogically, introductory courses in engineering, business and law should become part of core curricula leading to the B.A. and B.S. degrees. In these curricula they should receive time and attention equal to that accorded courses in the humanities and the social and natural sciences. They should be structured not only to impart the basic principles and benefits of disciplines but also to focus on the possible limitations, excesses and dangers inherent in each pursuit. Needless to say, similar caveats should be developed in the traditional arts and sciences.

How could these new courses be fitted into a student's schedule? I suggest by a reduction in electives. Admittedly, this is a sacrifice, but if courses in material culture are humanistic and well designed, they might be attractive electives in and of themselves. What do I mean by humanistic and well designed? I mean that courses dealing with technology, commerce and law should be more than technical introductions: they should be historical and comprehensive, weaving the subject at hand into the fabric of culture.

Though such a curricular restructuring would be vast and arduous, it would exploit existing resources rather than necessitating new investments. Once in place, it would offer an instructional spectrum that would go far in equipping American college students for active life.

INSTITUTIONAL REFORMS, GLOBAL IMPLICATIONS

What practicable first steps could lead to the development of such a new curriculum? A large university, comprising a college of arts and sciences and several professional schools, could handle this challenge flexibly and economically by establishing programs involving two or more schools but centered in the four-year college. Programs in commerce and law, Renaissance studies or the history of technology and design are examples of such outreach, while a program entitled "Modern Culture" might involve faculty from many schools — medicine, agriculture, law, business, engineering, education, architecture, fine arts, music, urban planning, etc. — in a single interdisciplinary venture. Smaller campuses would face a stiffer test, involving a degree of retooling (e.g., releasing time for professors to broaden their teaching scope) and a redirection of hiring priorities.

Such initiatives are likely to meet with opposition from departments that argue that releasing time for interdisciplinary programs or course development will rob them of the ability to run their majors. But this obstacle can be surmounted if the interdisciplinary programs *develop their own majors,* thus easing the departmental burden of undergraduate instruction. This step would have the simultaneous advantage of providing undergraduates with innovative and practical degree alternatives.

Let me conclude by noting that curricular reforms such as these look especially interesting in the light of the globalizing trends projecting through the 1990s and well into the twenty-first century. Examples such as recent Russian and Yugoslavian history make it painfully clear that prospering democratic institutions do not spring up monolithically but rather are available, if at all, only through comprehensive cultural renewal. If the United States is to make an active contribution to such an international renewal, it will be through the work of professionals who are cognizant of the interdependent currents of culture rather than through tunnel-sighted specialists. World citizenship will make interdisciplinary, even holistic demands, and we should be ready for them.

9

Eloquence, Controversy
and Silence

In 1986 a professor named Allan Bloom set the academic and publishing establishments back on their heels with a book called *The Closing of the American Mind,* a lively attack on the alleged spinelessness of American higher education, from a perspective largely derived from the thought of pagan antiquity. Bloom generated major surprise on two fronts: he shocked the academic community by exposing the low moral standards of its undergraduate curricula, and he shocked the publishing community by proving, for the first time in years, that an articulate philosophical book could be a bestseller.

It is worth noting that the two surprises generated by Bloom's book are contextually related to each other. Purposelessness in higher education and the relative rarity of philosophy in the public forum are both symptomatic of a society whose discourse is distorted down narrow professional channels rather than allowed free scope. In such a society major questions, like those concerning love, liberty, death and the function of higher education, go largely unaddressed; students are not educated, nor are professors qualified, to handle such questions. The major issues of life are considered "too general" by our academic specialists. In this light

Bloom's book functioned as a kind of wakeup call. It not only reminded us that the reading public can handle philosophical discourse. It reminded us that, responsibly and learnedly managed, philosophical discourse can awaken social self-knowledge.

This last point is of critical importance here. Throughout this book we have seen dialogic processes sharpening, sophisticating, liberating human awareness. With Bloom we see the reinstatement (if only temporary) of one of the most important dialogic loops of all: the reciprocity between authentic philosophical discourse and a public readership. Such a feedback not only gives society the unique opportunity to review and possibly redesign its institutions; it also opens a forum for an infinite variety of inquiries, insights and debates. While other professional studies are limited in their purviews, philosophy is the study of everything that matters.

This last statement may bring howls of derision from students of philosophy. *The study of everything that matters?* With few exceptions, our university philosophy departments have never studied any such thing.[69] For most of our "philosophers" there are only two subjects that matter: the history of philosophy, which they teach and write about, and the specialized subject matter of their current research. They would regard the idea that philosophy should treat everything that matters as hopelessly impractical. Yet I make the statement in spite of them, in order to support a theory. My theory is that if philosophers *were* educated to inquire into everything that matters and instructed on how to share this inquiry, not only with each other but also with the literate public, the world would be a livelier place and there would be many more good books to read.

This theory is based on two premises. In the first place, al-

---

69. Martin Buber and Alfred North Whitehead are two notable exceptions. See note 32.

though philosophy has been put to a variety of historical uses, it has served society in only two real ways: by sharpening the edge of thought, and by effectively treating topics of legitimate concern. In the second place, no topic that is or ought to be of legitimate concern to society should be beneath the notice of philosophers. They should discuss the other arts and sciences. They should explore society and politics. They should offer their own special insights into the order of nature and the ways of daily life.

If we go so far as to make this a definite item on our philosophical shopping list, then a second item is also essential. Philosophers should endeavor to make both their public and (insofar as possible) their professional utterances in clear, idiomatic language, free of neologism, jargon and nicety. After all, the discussion of things that matter concerns urgent things: oppression, suffering, sympathy, love, pain. We are all smack in the middle of, and share equally, a human situation that is real enough (if not a little too real) for any rational sensibility. Philosophers should face this reality squarely and simply.

Perhaps this is asking too much. After all, do our lawyers follow justice, our pastors virtue, our doctors health? Professional groups seem destined, as though by genetic coding, to fall away from original purposes and become purposes unto themselves. Yet from time to time perceived enormities lead to institutional reform. Perhaps the dawn of an information age — an age when all kinds of information, including professional publications, will be available for home viewing — will cause philosophers to reassess the nature of their communication with society.

Something of this sort happened in the Renaissance. Critical of the existing literary power structure, philosophically minded people started writing in the vernacular, and their writing turned from the traditional academic topics to subjects like pleasure, education, art, science, politics and the family. Finding their model in Cicero, who more than any other individual united philosophical insight with public policy, Renaissance humanists gave their new-found expressiveness the Latin name *eloquentia,* eloquence. Through eloquence they could bring innovative thought to a wide audience. Through eloquence they could renew society.[70]

This new informality of discourse and broadening of scope had momentous results, contributing to the modern idea of the individual, the invention of the essay and the birth of social science. More than any other single movement, humanism can be given credit for the rise of a free press and the development of democratic institutions in the West. But the diversity of interest that originally gave the movement its power ultimately divided its energies, and humanism, through its very success, slowly changed from an engine of social renewal to an array of academic, literary and political institutions. Moreover, as I pointed out in Chapter 5, the rise to dominance of the huge city and the resultant formation of a mass market and mass culture have isolated philosophical writing from the broader social forum, and a similar erosion of communicative channels has been effected by the increasing specialization of professional fields. Most writers, gifted or not, write in special languages for special audiences; those few who do not are hidden away on philosophy or self-help shelves in bookstores. Its social channels dry, eloquence must express itself in salable commodities or else rest mute and lonely in its possessor's heart.

This brings us again to Allan Bloom. Bloom made eloquence salable by appealing to a latent dissatisfaction (among the conservative and nonaligned) with the process of higher education. He drove home his critique with a strategy that was at once bold and refreshing: an appeal to Greek and Roman antiquity. But despite its colossal sales, his book had little effect on education. Why? There seem to be three main reasons.

Narrowness of View. A philosopher, Bloom believed that the

---

70. Excellent resources on this topic can be found in Trinkaus, *The Scope of Renaissance Humanism,* pp. 52–139; Murphy, *Renaissance Eloquence;* and Kennedy, *Classical Rhetoric,* pp. 195–219.

intellectual history of the modern world had been written by other philosophers — Rousseau, Hegel, Marx, Nietzsche, etc. — who had, without outside assistance, created modern values, the modern university and the modern mind. He ignored, or simply was not interested in, the idea of intellectual change as a social continuum, fueled not by a single discipline but rather by a variety of factors in public policy, economics, science, technology and art. This was a bad mistake. Rousseau did not invent unjust rulers, nor Marx oppressive employers; and the idea that God is dead owes more to the scientists Copernicus, Galileo and Darwin than it does to the philosopher Nietzsche or his followers. Neither did Bloom view the university in its full socioeconomic continuum; he saw it rather as a singular subject of criticism. These isolating tendencies gave *The Closing of the American Mind* an intellectualized, unrealistic quality which robbed it of social impact.

Overselling Antiquity. Bloom suggested that the classical world held values demonstrably superior to modern values. He withheld negative data about the classical period — details of widespread slavery, oppression and ignorance, data suggesting that things like philosophy were even more unpopular with most people back then than they are with most people now. Rather than offering the equipment for change, he left his reader in a mood of rather speciously induced nostalgia.

Failure to Call on Current Strengths. Lacking a comprehensive perspective, Bloom failed to tap into current strengths that might have materially advanced his cause and benefited higher education in the bargain. He did not note the increasing emphasis by corporate employers on dialogic skills. He ignored the resurgence of classical models in modern science and the congenial implications of environmentalism. He did not take into account the possibility that the communications revolution of 1980s and 1990s would stimulate reform by increasing the visibility and accountability of educators. Because he did not avail himself of these potential strengths, Bloom failed to suggest social receptor sites to which his vision of proper education might be attached.

The pluses and minuses of Bloom's book can teach us something about eloquence. If writers are to close the dialogic loop between philosophy and the reading public, they must address needs, conscious or lurking, in the minds of a substantial readership. They must handle issues with a sense of the continuity between and interdependency of social phenomena. They must tap into developing strengths, thus steering, rather than trying to arrest, the momentum of history.

SATIRE AS ELOQUENCE

On March 2, 1993, President Bill Clinton visited members of the Republican opposition in the Senate to discuss his program for economic reform and was ceremoniously presented by the senators with a check for $250 "to help him construct his new jogging trail at the White House." The joke was pretty obvious, based on the stereotype of Democrats as big spenders and Republicans as advocates of thrift. With the ironic gesture, amiable yet barbed, of a simple bank check, the Republicans had entered into history, as an inscribed check, one of the briefest documents of satire ever written.

Satire is everywhere in a free society, popping up graphically, audibly and literarily in almost all media of communication. Generally its target is established power: authorities, vested interests, institutions, professions and their assorted dogmas. Satire attacks these forms of power, usually by exaggerating their salient characteristics. In so doing, it implies that it emanates from higher moral ground and operates as a force of renewal.

Satire is generally topical and journalistic, but in some cases it can be lasting and eloquent. Jonathan Swift's *Gulliver's Travels* is one such case. I noted above that eloquence (philosophical writing for a broad readership) can only be effective if it taps into areas of conscious interest ("receptor sites") in society. Though Bloom accurately criticized American education and appealed to readers' unexpressed frustrations, he failed to address such strengths and thus did not fully complete his mission. Swift, in comparison, owed his brilliant success to having gained access to two such sites: his readers' delight in narrative and their fascination with the idea of reason.

Swift's classic tale, with its giants and midgets, its talking horses and apelike human beings, can tell us much about the power of satiric narrative. The narrative structure itself, with its exciting and entangling fictive events, is an engine of emotional force, pulling the reader into the discourse. Beguiled into attentiveness by these charms, the reader is then subjected to a number of destabilizing shocks. Clownish figures show gross similarities to reigning Western monarchs, savage rituals to time-honored Western traditions, monstrous abnormality to customary practice. Human dignity itself, a deep-seated assumption and a stable premise in the normal writer-reader relationship, is brutally impugned. Enfolded in the power of narrative, Swift's readers are subjected to a disquieting revelation, a monstrous awakening. They are compelled to recognize, in the dunderheaded behavior of his characters, unreasonable observances of their own.[71]

Gulliver's Travels provides us with an incident that is itself an eloquent metaphor for satiric art. Attached to the royal Lilliputian court, Gulliver awakens one night to a thousand cries of alarm. The palace is on fire! Our hero eagerly rushes to the scene and tries to help, only to find his progress in fighting the flames impeded by

---

71. One of Swift's ablest interpreters in our time was Allan Bloom himself. See his essay "Giants and Dwarfs: An Outline of *Gulliver's Travels*," in his *Giants and Dwarfs*, pp. 33–54.

a lack of water (the buckets are only "about the Size of a large Thimble"). Then Gulliver has a bright idea:

> I had the Evening before drank plentifully of a most delicious Wine, called *Glimigrim,* (the *Blefuscians* call it *Flunec,* but ours is esteemed the better Sort) which is very diuretick. By the luckiest Chance in the World, I had not discharged myself of any Part of it. The Heat I had contracted by coming very near the Flames, and by my labouring to quench them, made the Wine begin to operate by Urine; which I voided in such a Quantity, and applied so well to the proper Places, that in three Minutes the Fire was wholly extinguished; and the rest of that noble Pile, which had cost so many Ages in erecting, preserved from Destruction.[72]

Gulliver's helpful but embarrassing act symbolizes the social function of satire. Satire can only heal social ills (put out the fire) by offending, and its offense is particularly galling because the target is "the proper Places" — the ills that society most wants to hide. The better the satire is, the worse it makes people feel. For saving the palace, Gulliver is rewarded with an indictment for high treason.

CONTROVERSY

Satire functions as a kind of halfway point between eloquence and controversy. Controversy is an ambiguous element in social dialogue, because in and of itself it is nondialogic. Controversy imitates mechanical interaction: it is a nondevelopmental clash of firmly held viewpoints which struggle for dominance or survival. Group A says that there ought to be abortions. Group B says that

---

72. *Gulliver's Travels,* Book I, Chapter 5.

there ought not to be abortions. The positions, the reasoning and the rhetoric do not change for years. There is no place for teaching or eloquence in controversy: both sides already know their own particular truth. Successful controversy requires determination and debating skills; receptive intelligence is a drawback.

Why then is controversy an element in evolving social dialogue? First of all, because controversy publicizes an issue, thus becoming in spite of itself a factor in the dialogic flow of information through society. While the lords of controversy may be confirmed and immovable, nonaligned people outside the fray, hearing about the issue through news of this debate or that harangue, are likely to be more thoughtful: capable, someday, of productive change. Second, controversy takes on dialogic features when portrayed in a magnified time scale. Positions, be they Catholic and Protestant, Arab and Israeli, Afrikaner and black South African, *do* alter slowly by exposure to each other, especially after the standoff of controversy gives way to the process of negotiation. The statement of one group, the answer of another, dissolve into a grand feedback process which Hegel gave the dialogic name of "dialectic."[73]

SILENCE

The deadly alternative to eloquence and controversy is silence. By silence I mean the moral inertia of masses of people who, for whatever reason, are not inquiring into their own condition or acknowledging the existence of issues. In tyrannies, this inertia is usually the result of subjection and depression; in free societies, it is brought on by complacency, top-heavy leadership and undevel-

73. On controversy in philosophy and its relation to dialogue, see Richard McKeon's essay, "Dialogue and Controversy in Philosophy," in Maranao's *The Interpretation of Dialogue,* pp. 25–46.

oped communicative systems. When Allan Bloom published *The Closing of the American Mind,* he was actually attacking *two* positions: liberal educators who did not believe in the teaching of values, and *silent* educators who did not believe in anything at all but simply went about their business in a moral vacuum. And while the liberal position, like it or not, makes for some profitable discussion, the silent position is brainsick and dangerous. Silence annuls the élan of free societies, which feed on issues for their alertness and endurance. Silence bespeaks a human passion convenient to tyrants but hurtful to democracies, referred to in Chapter 6 as the passion to be left alone and vegetate. Silence is the denial of dialogue, or rather its disestablishment, for the silent masses, morally sterile themselves, bequeath nothing to the young except stupidity and acquiescence.

If dialogue is the lifeblood of free society, silence is the dark polarity, the desperate consequence of failure to understand or meet the challenges of liberty.

Personal Eloquence

The distinction between "honesty" and "rhetoric" is traditional and customary. Rhetoric is supposed to be indirect and artful; honesty, direct and artless. But this distinction tends to wear thin when we remember that all discourse, spoken or written, has distinct and palpable form. What we see and think and feel must be translated into words, and this translation is a creative process. Thus even honesty uses a kind of art, and the person speaking honestly must be as alert and convincing as the salespitcher or the liar.

What is the rhetoric of honesty? Better ask, what is honesty itself? To my mind, honesty is less an urge to tell the truth (for the dishonest know how to use truth) than *a disposition and urge to tell all* — to express and share without stint or pretense or omission the full sweep of one's experience and feeling. Thus honesty, which is itself a quest for wholeness, is ideally expressed by a wholeness of discourse, by speech or text that is rich in tonalities and perspectives. Consequently, copia (Chapter 3) would seem to constitute the rhetoric of honesty.

But copia is not the rhetoric of everyday life. Everyday interactions — specific questions and requests, expressions of or appeals for affection, resolutions of disagreement, etc. — do not allow for abundant and varied response. Neither, of course, do they allow for a direct expression of how we happen to be feeling at the moment; this might be shocking and hurtful. We therefore construct, for social purposes, a personal language of the constant self: a language that in responding to immediate challenges nonetheless reflects long-term values and commitments. This personal language is our version of eloquence. It translates our identity for the world.

But the fact that personal eloquence is an art form, and indeed a fragile one, is made clear to many of us every day. It does not take an earthquake or a murder or fierce social uproar to shatter one's constructed self; returning to family life in one's own home is often sufficient. In a family containing at least one child, language becomes subject to quasi-seismic stresses, and presumed identity can crumble into gibberish.

Family-induced stresses on language include catharsis and catatonia. Catharsis occurs because children are going through a long and slow socialization process at school and need someone to punish for it. Without proper guidance they will turn their home into an emotional dump, scapegoating other family members and converting publicly concealed frustrations into private atrocities. Catharsis drives siblings and often parents into catatonia. As we listen to a family member release emotional tension, a great silence creeps into us, as though our blood vessels were open to the tide of a rapidly freezing sea. Catatonia also results from the realization that no matter how interesting or important a subject one brings up, one's family may respond with cathartic derision or outrage.

Together, catharsis and catatonia bring on the ultimate decline of eloquence, of communication itself, into irrelevance. There is nothing at all chaotic about this irrelevance; rather, it consists of the strict rule that only trivia and blather will be considered acceptable discourse, while the expression of personal discoveries or heartfelt concerns will be punished in direct proportion to its urgency. Families afflicted by irrelevance become the images of dysfunctional nations, where institutions have broken down, authorities exist for their own sake and nothing rational is tolerated. In such a setting, only irrelevance offers the hope of survival.

There is no way out of this morass except very hard work. The work begins in one-on-one dialogues between family members. Privacy tends to relieve the symptoms of catharsis and catatonia and thus to open the way for dialogue. But creating this opening is not enough. Children and sometimes adults too lack a vocabulary of emotion that will allow them to recognize, understand and express their own feelings. This vocabulary must illuminate two key distinctions, the distinction between the temporary and the permanent (e.g., between the question of who gets a new bicycle and the ongoing dynamics of sibling relationships) and the distinction between personal inclinations and the family commonwealth. Beyond this the vocabulary must equip children and parents to express their concerns dialogically rather than antagonistically. Children must learn the simple eloquence of honesty and commitment.[74]

Progress in this direction is typically slow. In particular, the inner tyrannies of adolescence may narrow the lines of dialogue to a thread. But if you speak earnestly, children may listen to you even during the uproar of disagreement, and you may someday be surprised to hear them communicate the power of dialogue to their juniors.

---

74. There are many studies of communicative processes in the family. See, for example, Tannen, *You Just Don't Understand;* Rusk, *The Power of Ethical Persuasion;* Sieburg, *Family Communication;* Galvin, *Family Communication;* and Verderber, *Communicate!*

PART THREE

DIALOGUE AND FREEDOM
IN SCIENCE AND
PHILOSOPHY

IO

❧❧❧

The Dialogue of
Science and Nature

Discussing diversity in Chapter 8, I wrote that "diversity and redundancy suggest to us that nature, as well as mind and society, behaves dialogically and can be examined as dialogue." My purpose in characterizing nature as dialogue was not to create a striking metaphor, or even to discover an evocative similarity. Rather, I meant to express the conviction that human dialogue is itself but a tiny aspect of natural interactions that are every bit as reciprocal and evolutionary as dialogue is. Though oral and written dialogue have elevated us above the other species, these skills do not demarcate us from the rest of nature but show our continuity with it. Through dialogue we can imitate nature's ways. Through dialogue we can inquire into nature's workings.

What sort of dialogue makes inquiry into nature possible? A sort, I would have to say, rather different from anything we have looked at yet. Up to this point we have explored aspects of dialogic thought that are morally renewing and socially liberating. Modern natural science is neither of these things. Indeed, the attitude and method unique to modern science would be corrupted by such considerations. Though science obviously can work for good or evil, its operative method must be politically unconscious, morally blind. Yet science is dialogic in a way that other disciplines can only envy. Science conducts a dialogue with nature.

The media for this dialogue are the two staples of scientific inquiry, hypothesis and experiment. Hypothesis is an abstract initiative, experiment a concrete realization. Hypothesis is the platform, experiment the support.

HYPOTHESIS

In science the hypothetical method is a way of testing a new idea. The idea, if deemed worthy of trial, is established as an imaginary reality and questioned in terms of its necessary consequences. Such questioning is best described as "If . . . , then . . . ," with "If . . ." being the hypothesis itself and "then . . ." being the consequences. To test a hypothesis effectively, researchers must think copiously, exhausting insofar as possible the conclusions that must follow if the hypothesis is correct. Such testing is patient and merciless, involving every applicable contingency. If a single consequence does not apply, the hypothesis as stated is faulty and cannot be established.[75]

The dialogic character of hypothesis is vaguely reminiscent of the phenomena discussed in Chapter 4, "The Dialogue of Invention." Writers create manuscripts which, as they grow in length, increasingly assert their own autonomy and separateness, engaging the writers in a dialogic feedback. In scientific hypothesis, researchers have ideas which *they deliberately force away from them-*

---

75. Or, as Paul T. Durbin puts it under the heading "Hypothetico-Deductive Method," "If some hypothesis (H) is true, then certain observable facts (O) can be expected; if the facts (O) are found to be as predicted, H is confirmed to some degree" (*Dictionary of Concepts in the Philosophy of Science,* p. 123). For a classic treatment of hypothesis, see Poincaré, *The Foundations of Science,* Chapter 9. On the origins of the hypothetical method, see Cassirer, "Galileo's Platonism."

selves, objectifying them and submitting them to a variety of questions. Both procedures depend on a splitting of perspective, an acknowledgment of the "otherness" of one's own idea, and a feedback interaction with it. The divorce of self from self and the resultant communion of self with self are thus characteristic of both methods. But here the resemblance ends. Writers can play with their creations, emphasizing certain strengths and associations at the expense of others, to the manifest end of delighting and/or enlightening readers. Scientists, in contrast, must prove their theses via objective and comprehensive analysis to the dispassionate eye of science itself. Thus arises the paradox that science is at once more powerful than the other arts and less liberating.

EXPERIMENT

I sit in a University of California classroom listening to my University of Oregon colleague Peter von Hippel give a guest lecture to graduate students in molecular biology. Again and again, in detailing his position on a complex and controversial issue, he speaks of his lab's activities in terms of interrogation: "We ask when . . . ," "We ask whether . . . ," "We ask how much . . ." In each case the word "ask" denotes a formal experiment, conducted under ground rules so exacting that once published, it never needs to be conducted again. Von Hippel's description of experimenting as asking is common among scientists and completely appropriate. An experiment is a question we ask of nature. If the question is properly designed and enunciated, nature will respond with the information that we request.

Such questions are like works of art. To ask them correctly, scientists must be more than precise and meticulous: they must be imaginative, fair and self-depreciating. They must envisage exactly what sort of information they need to discover and invent a means by which it will be made explicit. They must temporarily submerge their preconceptions, their expectations, their very identity. They must become silent so that only nature speaks. By using the word "ask," von Hippel is not only describing a procedure but conveying an attitude. This attitude might be called a technical chivalry, a courtesy of expertise, a humility toward experience.

How do experiments "ask"? An experiment is a controlled event in which irrelevant variables are suppressed and relevant variables are allowed to function freely. These relevant variables must be made to function in a way that can be monitored accurately. This combination of restricted scope and free function and accuracy of observation provides a window into the forces of nature at work.

COMMUNICATION IN SCIENCE

Other dialogic interactions foster discovery at von Hippel's laboratory. At weekly meetings, members of the laboratory staff present their own recent research to their colleagues and are questioned by them about it. These presentations not only keep staff members alert to the activities of the laboratory as a whole but also allow for essential networking, double-checking and troubleshooting. The very architecture of Streisinger Hall, the building that houses the laboratory, encourages dialogue with its large open spaces and numerous nooks and alcoves along its corridors.

The impressive openness and vitality of dialogue in von Hippel's laboratory is paralleled by communicative processes in the scientific community as a whole. In Chapter 5 I called science "utopian in its communicative philosophy" and compared its discursive openness with the narrow and clogged channels of bureaucracy. Let me briefly review this topic in the new context provided here.

Scientific communication is excellent because scientific journals are committed to publishing only genuine innovations, and genu-

ine innovations characteristically empower all observers who understand them. A step forward for one scientist is thus a step
forward for all scientists; the individual good and the common
good intersect; advantage and virtue coincide. Because of these
factors, because of the relative speed of publication in the sciences
and because of the international applicability of scientific nota-
tion, the interval between making a real contribution and being
honored for it is significantly shorter than in other disciplines. Of
course these virtues are limited by human frailty: some scientists
will envy the achievements of others; some will borrow without
asking or acknowledging; some will put on airs; some will misuse
authority or pander to it; some will even fake results. But the
modus operandi of science discourages such vices. Science, which
thrives on nature's honesty, breeds honesty in its acolytes.

Similarly, dialogue and criticism are more effective in science
than in other modes of inquiry. Because of the intersection of
individual and common good, scientists tend to see all criticism as
self-criticism; that is, they challenge or criticize the theories of
others in a basically sympathetic effort to improve them. A familiar scientific witticism goes, "When we don't like somebody, we
don't criticize his or her work." This attitude is to a considerable
extent mirrored in the way in which scientists *take* helpful criticism. The ethic of *asking* and *learning*, pursued so effectively in
scientists' dealings with nature, inheres in their dealings with one
another.

Can other disciplines learn anything from these outstandingly
dialogic propensities? I think they can. Using natural science as a
standard, humanists and social scientists should foster what might
be called a colloquial mentality, a set of values and proceedings
framed on the essentially dialogic nature of productive thought.
This would mean, first of all, an enhancement of colloquial media
via the creation of new journals, newsletters and network discussion groups allowing for speedy publication and broadening the
range of valid expression to include interdisciplinary, self-critical

and creative initiatives. Second, scholarship would benefit from the deprivatization of research: interactive inquiries — symposiums, retreats, faculty seminars — should receive increased emphasis, while articles and books written about recondite topics, intended chiefly as assertions of authority and directed to tiny audiences, should receive diminished credit. Third, the ethic of asking and learning should be fostered by requiring scholars of all ages to seek instruction in areas outside their own fields, thus reminding them that they are students throughout their careers, and by bolstering collegial interaction between scientists and nonscientists.

THE DIALOGIC POWER OF SCIENCE
AND CONNECTED QUESTIONS

The rise of modern science and its attendant technologies dates back to the era (the seventeenth century) when hypothesis and experiment became widely accepted tools in a socially endorsed project. These essentially dialogic strategies so profoundly empowered natural science that it speedily became a more influential force of social evolution than any other learned field. Inquirers into the human realm — historians, philologists, philosophers, political thinkers, etc. — have long stood in awe of scientists and often tried to imitate their methods. Typically they fall short, for while philosophical and social inquiry addresses a field full of change, paradox and ambiguity, scientific questions are addressed to a subject that never changes or lies.[76] Nature's truth-telling has

---

76. The distinction between "precise" and "imprecise" disciplines was first articulated by Plato (in the *Philebus,* 55e–58e) and Aristotle (*Nichomachean Ethics,* I.iii), but the crown for precision was not awarded to natural science until the new science of the Renaissance and seventeenth century.

made modern scientific inquiry incrementally progressive, while inquiry in other fields wanders and wavers, halts and restarts.

But in this very knowledge gap between science and the humanities lurks a surprising conundrum. Science may well be a more powerful pursuit than inquiry into human affairs, but isn't science itself a human affair, and as such a subject of inquiry? Can we ask science questions about itself, and if so, how will we frame them? We cannot test hypotheses about science or experiment on it. Yet confront it we must. As the most powerful — and hence potentially the most dangerous — of all human initiatives, natural science must be included in a philosophical and political rationale.

Since the philosophical evaluation of science cannot be made scientifically, it must emerge, like other speculative and moral initiatives, from the prison of subjectivity and the rag-and-bone shop of the humanities and social sciences. The ideal evaluator would to some extent imitate the natural scientist, for the humility, attentiveness, simplicity and candor of science have long been missed in other fields. But while science is committed to the self-limiting dialogue of hypothesis and experiment, the evaluator of science should follow a more copious dialogue, which does science full credit but places it in the bustling variety of human perspectives.

THE DIALOGUE OF SCIENCE AND SOCIETY

Such an evaluation might begin as follows.

Obviously science tells us about nature, but it is worth a moment to consider what sorts of things it tells us and why we want to know them. To the ancients (the Pre-Socratics, Plato, Aristotle), science was purely speculative: a branch of philosophy whose goals did not extend beyond understanding and teaching. Even the brilliant engineer Archimedes considered himself first and foremost a philosopher and belittled his own technological achievements. With a single notable exception — the alchemists — this distinction persisted through the Middle Ages. All this changed in the Renaissance. Early Renaissance humanism equated knowledge and art with power, and Machiavelli radicalized this equation by showing that power had no intrinsic relationship to a Christian moral framework. At the same time Paracelsus, schooled in the hermetic tradition of the alchemists, was laying the groundwork for modern chemistry and asserting that natural science could be a source of limitless power.[77] Early in the seventeenth century this assertion and its corollaries were set out in detail by Francis Bacon, whose ideas helped bring about the formation of the Royal Society and the rise of science as a significantly supported enterprise.[78]

This intellectual revolution not only empowered science but recast it as a *facilitative* rather than *contemplative* discipline. Science was thus effectively divorced from philosophy and permanently allied to technology and commerce. To appreciate this alliance, we need only reflect on the fact that currently the vast majority of active laboratory scientists work for industry, while the vast majority of academic scientists envision practical results for their research.

Why is this history relevant? Because the essentially facilitative function of science necessarily characterizes and limits the dialogue between science and society. Scientists' loyal pursuit of the truth about nature is part of an enormous project of social empowerment. Science tells society *what society wants to know about*

---

77. Paracelsus taught that human insight into nature was potentially unlimited because divine wisdom was inborn in humanity (see Jacobi, *Paracelsus: Selected Writings*, pp. 127–40).

78. For Bacon's contribution to the rise of modern science, see particularly his *New Organon (Novum Organum)*, his *Proficience and Advancement of Learning* and his *New Atlantis*, all of which exist in numerous editions. On the Royal Society, see Purver, *The Royal Society.*

nature, and what society wants to know — medicine, energy, production, communications — is what will give it power. Science does not offer us wisdom; it puts tools in our hands. But it does so with such express and elegance that we often mistake its limited offerings for the whole truth.

To acknowledge this limitation in science is to recognize the need for expanded dialogue between science and society via a speculative discipline that is conversant with science but not included in it.[79]

SUMMARY

Science has outdistanced other modes of inquiry because scientists have developed effective dialogic means of communicating with nature and with one another. But science cannot ask questions about itself. And because the mission of science is limited to empowerment, science does not consider all the questions about nature that are relevant.

THOUGHTS ABOUT NATURE AND DIALOGUE

Dialectical Nature. The Pre-Socratics Heraclitus and Parmenides were dialectic naturalists. Heraclitus taught that all natural phenomena derived from the interaction of opposite forces, which condemned the world to ceaseless and comprehensive change. Parmenides taught that strife and love were the two main forces of

---

79. Studies of science and society abound. Among the more comprehensive are Crowther, *Science in Modern Society,* and Needham, *The Great Titration.* Also see Gadamer, *Reason in the Age of Science;* Leiss, *The Domination of Nature;* and Schwartz, *The Creative Moment.*

nature, that love fostered stability while strife fomented change. A modern equivalent for the Parmenidean dualism might be found in "strong" nuclear forces, which bind subatomic particles together, and "weak" forces, which push them away from each other. On a chemical or biochemical scale, the dualism might be compared with positive-feedback, morphogenetic chemical processes (as described by Ilya Prigogine), as opposed to entropy (chaotic forces or level of chaos).

∾ *Reductionism vs. Holism.* A not unrelated issue has been the subject of sporadic debate among scientists since the 1960s. Natural science is traditionally reductive, proceeding on the premise that if we can understand the essential components of nature, we can understand all their more complicated interactions with one another. Fighting a viral infection, science seeks to understand the way in which viruses enter human cells, why the cells do not resist them, what they do there and, even more microscopically, what their genetic makeup is. Holistic science, however, takes the whole organism, or even a group of organisms, as the basic unit of study. The holistic premise is that comprehensive feedback interactions determine the activity and hence the character of individual components. As Stuart Kauffman puts it in the preface to his recent book *At Home in the Universe,* "The complex whole may exhibit properties that are not readily explained by understanding the parts."[80] Thus holistic medicine is less interested in the structure of viruses or the composition of drugs than in strengthening the

---

80. Pp. vii–viii. The classic statement of holism in science is Koestler and Smythies' *Beyond Reductionism,* including essays by F. A. von Hayek, Jean Piaget and Viktor Frankl. *At Home in the Universe* proceeds to specify and describe a number of instances of morphogenesis within apparently chaotic systems. Kauffman does not mention Koestler or Smythies, though like them he draws some of his method from systems theory.

body's natural defenses against disease.[81] The merits of both holistic science and reductive science are obvious, though there is no reason that one of them should be seen as necessarily canceling out the other.

The Environment as Dialogic Nature. Erasmus, who taught Europe about the idea of copia, remarked that nature itself is copious in its provision of wondrous variety (*De copia,* I.viii). The idea of nature as copia is relevant today in at least two ways. First, the diversity of life must be preserved so that the biosphere can maintain its subtle balances and so that ecosystems can respond to change. Second, we must learn to think copiously about nature, to understand that many natural phenomena — the action of an organ, the behavior of a predator, the chemistry of a body of water — are functions of many simultaneous forces. Aldo Leopold had this in mind when he instructed his readers to "think like a mountain": to understand as a living unity all the subtly and sometimes paradoxically interactive forces at work in a single area.[82]

Anti-dialogic Aspects of Science. The idea of copia should remind us that important topics are not fully considered or engaged unless we have access to them from the full variety of valid perspectives. Here it must be admitted that natural science falls short. Reductive tendencies in science and the experimental necessity for limiting subjectivity and nonessential variables give the scientific mind a monistic cast. Scientists are ill at ease with ambiguity; similarly, they tend to settle into productive methodologies (e.g., reductivism or holism) without considering that alternative and even antithetical methodologies might also be productive. These propensities in part account for the lack of self-inquiry described earlier in

---

81. See Dienstrey, *Where Mind Meets Body.* Dienstrey is editor of *Advances* (published by the Fetzer Institute), a journal addressing mind/body wellness.

82. "Thinking Like a Mountain," in *A Sand County Almanac.* Also see Susan Flader's *Thinking Like a Mountain.*

this chapter, and the combination of limited perspective and dramatic practical success has endowed some scientists, notably physicists, with an unbecoming vanity.

What Science Does Not Study. I noted above that modern science has concentrated on empowerment and not wisdom. It might fairly be asked, what sort of wisdom is science ignoring? I would answer that human power is often won at the expense of nature, and therefore that mere empowerment is barbaric and self-endangering. No scientific project is creditable unless it involves serious attention to environmental consequences, and no science student illiterate in the environment should receive a university degree. The programmatic incorporation of environmentalism into scientific education would not only civilize science; it would also enrich, temper and professionalize the environmental movement. Why should I call this wisdom? Because, as we learn from teachers like Aldo Leopold, environmentalism is grounded in the contemplation of nature's wisdom. Of the many questions that science asks nature, one that should be heard more often is "How can we live in greater harmony with you?"

Language and
Human Nature

I sit in my study on a fine morning in May, looking at my computer screen, which looks back at me, its once placid face now increasingly scarred with words, as though in communion. My computer, thank heavens, cannot get up and fend for itself, but in other important ways it is a kind of rough copy of me: its chief operative components are hardware (the circuitry, keyboard, screen, etc., which are sensitive to information) and software (information, introduced from outside, telling the hardware how to behave). As a human being, I am characterized by a functionally identical division. My hardware (senses, brain, nerves, etc.) receives, processes, responds to information, but it would be quite helpless to do this without my software (language, education, experience in general) to tell it how to operate. Just as my computer, with its large storage space and powerful memory, would be blank and stupid without programs to fill them, so I, without the benefit of lengthy, subtle learning processes, would be unable to think, to walk, to see.

This enormous dependency of hardware on software was underlined clinically quite recently. Oliver Sacks, a neurologist and writer, observed the behavior of a patient who had been blind since childhood and who was having his vision surgically restored. The results of this treatment were striking but quite similar to previous case studies. The patient recovered the hardware of vision but could not *see*. Depth and motion perception, object recognition — spatial understanding in general — eluded him. The mental processes of seeing, built incrementally in all of us by years of repeated experience from infancy, were at this stage of his life quite beyond reach.[83]

I cite this example to illustrate the profound extent to which our behavior, our character, our human nature itself are influenced by our experience and by the technologies we learn. The faculties of hearing, sight and touch, once assumed to be automatic, are not fully packaged gifts of nature. They are rather technologies: acquired tools for dealing with the world. Like the software that governs the hardware, they are keyed into us by experience or teaching or our own experimentation. We are not born human; we learn to be.

This is obviously the case with the two interrelated skills that crown our humanity, language and interpretive thought. These technologies, which so distinctly characterize us that the linguist Jean Aitchison can define our species as "the articulate mammal," are, like vision, learned rather than inborn. But unlike sight and walking, which seem to be more or less universalized, language and thought are highly variegated technologies. A metropolitan child educated at a private school will speak and think very differently from the child of a remote aboriginal tribe, and the distinc-

---

83. Sacks, "To See and Not See." Arthur Zajonc develops the same idea in his *Catching the Light* and concludes, "The sober truth remains that vision requires far more than a functioning physical organ. Without an inner light, without a formative visual imagination, we are blind" (see pp. 1–6). Recent research in physiology suggests that experience is so important in growth that the eye even "learns" to be nearsighted or farsighted. See Blakeslee, "Studies Offer a New Understanding of Myopia."

tion will be further radicalized when the metropolitan child avails himself or herself of writing, telephones and computers while the aboriginal child grows to maturity in an oral and preindustrial culture. The way we think — which is in effect the way we *are* — is deeply tied not only into our language structures but into the other communicative technologies we employ. This does not make one person more human than another, but it does underline the enormous diversity of social character.

Equally dramatic distinctions operate across time. Most modern languages are of relatively recent origin (English orthography, for example, remained irregular into the nineteenth century). Given the scope of human history and prehistory, writing itself is by no means an ancient invention. Human communication, revolutionalized by writing and then again by printing, has gone through a succession of dazzling changes in this century alone. Innovations of this order and profundity do not leave humanity unaffected. As communicative technologies develop, our character changes with them.

Language/thought differentiation over space and time is one of the reasons that, as I said in the preceding chapter, the study of human affairs cannot be conducted with scientific precision. The variables are too deeply interwoven with the constants, and on top of this, our means of inquiry will inevitably be tinted by the language/thought frame we currently inhabit. For these reasons alone, copious or multi-perspectival modes of analysis are more effective in human studies than narrowly controlled efforts to achieve singular truth. Copious thinking accepts, engages, imitates human variability. By the same token, we ought to be as copious in time as we are in attitude. Changing technologies demand constant reassessment. Each new interpretive generation must reexamine how it hears and sees.

II

⌍⌐⌍

The One and the Many:
The Dialogue of
Cognition

A man made a long pilgrimage to a holy city. As he neared the city he saw, looming above the lower, irregular shapes of other structures, the walls and roof of the great temple that was the object of his journey. Yet again and again, as he searched through dark narrow alleys and small marketplaces, he failed to find the entrance. As best he could in a language not his own, he made inquiries of the townspeople, but all of them, taught in a newer religion, seemed neither to know nor to care. After much frustration, he was directed at last to a priest of the old faith, who told him that the great temple had in fact long ceased to possess a formal entrance but rather could be entered in many ways, through any of the narrow houses and tiny shops that surrounded it. Yet in the end this revelation gave the pilgrim no help at all. Each house and shop he entered was so dark and squalid, its furniture so alien, its occupants so forbidding, that it seemed manifestly incapable of opening into the grandeur and freedom of the temple vault. The man left the city in bitterness and sought an easier faith.[84]

The image of the temple and the pilgrim has haunted me ever since it first appeared to me years ago. It speaks to me of a vivid paradox:

84. This parable concludes my *Time and the Art of Living.*

of the complete immediacy of spiritual truth and its utter remoteness. It reminds me that I cannot have access to essential experience (the temple vault) unless I am fully conversant with trivial experience (the many little doorways); that I cannot apprehend Unity without having embraced Multiplicity; that I cannot hear a whisper of the eternal while turning a deaf ear to the everyday. And it suggests, finally, that this paradoxical interdependency of One and Many applies not only to the truth of the spirit but to any kind of truth at all.

This chapter discusses the One and the Many as essential elements in human cognition.

✧ Plato's dialogues have a history rich at once in passionate cherishing and total neglect. Preserved by his students in Greece, his works found their way to Constantinople; in the mid-fifteenth century, they were taken to Florence, where Cosimo ("Il Vecchio") de' Medici commissioned Marsilio Ficino to translate them into Latin. Their appearance in Ficino's highly readable edition exerted a profound influence on the thought of the time. During the Renaissance, and for the centuries following, the Platonic dialogue became the classic expression of idealism and philosophical spiritualism.

But the nature of this influence was scarcely what Plato himself would have wanted. In the course of his long career he drastically altered his perspective, moving from early and middle dialogues characterized by spiritualism and idealism *(Phaedo, Phaedrus, Symposium, Republic)* to late dialogues *(Parmenides, Sophist, Statesman, Philebus, Timaeus, Laws)* of a more moderate, if not conservative, bent. And as idealistic and spiritual themes lost prominence in his attention, so their spokesman, his great teacher, Socrates, faded from eminence in his dialogues. Plato was becoming his own man, moving away from the lyrical and often passionate description of absolutes and toward the evenhandedness, practicality and emphasis on method that would be so great an influence on his student Aristotle.

The Renaissance ignored all this. What excited Renaissance readers was what had excited the Neo-Platonists and the early Christians: Plato's unrivaled ability *to present idealized forms as though they were innate realities.* There was something thrilling, almost inebriating, about this for many readers, and besides, for the more jaded, it made Plato easy to disagree with and reject as an absolutist. Coupled with scholars' neglect of his other contributions, this emphasis effectively truncated the Platonic corpus, diminishing it from heroic philosophical status to the inaccurate but manageable shape we know today.

My mission in this chapter brings us into contact with the lost or "dead" Plato — the Plato familiar to only a small group of classicists and philosophers. We must look in fact at the dialogue in which Plato seems to have dramatized his own break with idealism, the *Parmenides.* This dialogue can teach us far more than the history of ideas. It can teach us about the essentially dialogic parameters of our own thought.

PLATO'S *PARMENIDES*

Summary: The young Socrates visits the venerable philosopher Parmenides and asks him to clarify a specific point relating to the theory of forms (quintessential abstract ideas like "the good" or "largeness"). Parmenides responds by questioning Socrates about forms in general (130b).[85] After a few questions and answers, it is clear to both speakers that the theory of forms is in

---

85. Instead of page numbers for the *Parmenides,* I am using a notational form from the manuscript tradition that is common in Greek editions and most translations. The translation is by F. M. Cornford in *The Collected Dialogues of Plato,* ed. Edith Hamilton and Huntington Cairns (Princeton: Princeton University Press, 1961).

big trouble: there is no clear and uncontradictory way of show-ing that forms exist or demonstrating their relationship to things of this world. Yet, as Parmenides briefly suggests in the end, forms are absolutely essential to the process of thinking (135b). Is there a way out of this conundrum? When Parmenides is convinced by his friends to take up the matter again, he engages it in the most general terms: *are phenomena unified ("One") or boundlessly diverse ("Many")?* If One, then unified forms like "the good" and "largeness" are credible; if Many, then neither these forms nor anything permanently nameable exists. Parmenides proceeds first to demolish the idea of the One and then (142b–) to rebuild it. He concludes this lesson in contra-diction with the absurdly inclusive statement "It seems that, whether there is or is not a one, both that one and the others alike are and are not, and appear and do not appear to be, all manner of things in all manner of ways, with respect to them-selves and to one another."

Plato's *Parmenides* is so abstract, so complicated, so self-defeat-ing and so inconclusive that some commentators take it to be self-parody. But this interpretation is certainly short of the mark. When Plato wishes to write parody or poke fun, he does so with a verve that illuminates every page.[86] Instead the *Parmenides* seems to be a kind of philosophical rite of passage: an effort by Plato to express his own ascent from one level of awareness to another. Until the *Parmenides,* Plato had sided with Socrates and the Pythagoreans in defending idealized forms (the One) against at-tacks by Heraclitus, the natural scientists and the Sophists, who saw phenomena as changeable and experience as diverse (the Many). Now he saw the question as more complex. Neither the

---

86. For parody in Plato, see Agathon's speech in the *Symposium* (194e–197e) and Lysias' speech, read by Phaedrus, in the *Phaedrus* (230e–234c). For other instances of humor in Plato, see the *Protagoras,* passim, and Aristophanes' speech in the *Sympo-sium* (189a–193e).

One nor the Many can be satisfactorily established. Each side must acknowledge the claims of the other. The answer does not lie in the solution of the issue. The issue is the answer.

In another late dialogue, the *Philebus*, Plato summarizes this discovery, calling it "a gift of the gods."[87]

THE *PARMENIDES* AND
THE DIALOGUE OF COGNITION

What does all this have to do with the nature of dialogue? A good question. Before answering it, let me look briefly at the implications for philosophers. The *Parmenides* makes two epochal discoveries. The first is that both radically monistic theorizing and radically relativistic theorizing are a waste of time. The second is that all truly reasonable interpretations of experience should partake of both monistic and relativistic perspectives. This spells doom for the optimistic theory, endorsed by Socrates and by the younger Plato, that philosophy can march in progressive stages to the doorway of absolute Unity and Truth.[88] Philosophy instead is condemned to a perpetuity of incertitude: to a lifetime spent negotiating a ceaseless stress between opposed perspectives.

But the implications of the *Parmenides* do not stop with formal philosophy. They extend to thought at large: to the ceaseless human project of interpreting reality. They suggest that to a large extent, we cannot find our way through life without depending on and acknowledging two contradictory perspectives. They posit

---

87. "All things, so it ran, that are ever said to be, consist of a one and a many, and have in their nature a conjunction of limit and unlimitness" (*Philebus*, 16d; translated by R. Hackforth in *The Collected Dialogues of Plato*, ed. Edith Hamilton and Huntington Cairns [Princeton: Princeton University Press, 1963]).

88. For a statement of this theory, see the *Symposium*, 210a–212c.

a dialogue of cognition, an elemental ambiguity in our mental structuring of experience.[89]

This ambiguity has its roots in the earliest conscious thought processes, recognition and language acquisition. Here the One and the Many, as similarity and distinctness, function as opposed but complementary faculties. As children we recognize objects — books, chairs, trees — equally by their similarity to one another and their distinctness from other kinds of objects. This process of combined similitude and distinction leads to an automated eye→brain response: seeing a chair, even one that we have never seen before, we accept it as a known presence. The idea of chair — chairness, if you will — is internalized, to the extent that it can be retrieved by the simple use of the word "chair" preceded by the indefinite article "a." "Bring me a chair, Nelly," says the child's parent. She obeys, miraculously solving the philosophical problem of abstract vs. concrete.

Similarity/distinctness interactions are at the heart of all ideas — and hence of all language, for every word is an idea of sorts. When as children we learn the word "go," we learn it as an idea of a *variety* of actions that are *united* among themselves and *distinct* from all others in their emphasis on deliberate motion. If we thought of one word as meaning all things (the One), or if we felt bound to apply a different word to each object or feeling we had (the Many), we would have no thought or language at all. It is only by combining the two opposite perspectives that we conceive and communicate. The basis of all dialogue — the essential dialogue, if you will — is the Dialogue of the One and the Many.

A related ambiguity inheres in more advanced forms of cogni-

---

89. Plato anticipates this cognitive distinction when he posits "same" and "other" as key elements in created nature (*Timaeus,* 35–40). I am grateful to Professor Malcolm Wilson for this observation.

tion. Early social thinkers such as Francis Bacon and Thomas Hobbes divided rational thinking into *connective* and *disjunctive* faculties. The connective faculty, which included metaphor and all other bringing-togethers, was commonly called "fancy"; the disjunctive faculty, which governed the recognition of distinctness, was known as "judgment." Fanciful people were very creative, always drawing connections; people of judgment were great at analyzing problems and trying cases. It was clear from experience that fancy and judgment had different psychological roots and appeared in different character types. People rich in fancy tended to be warm, liberal, emotional, loving; people rich in judgment tended to be dry, conservative, reserved, canny.[90]

DEEPER ASSOCIATIONS

But such distinctions only scratch the surface. The One/Many dichotomy expresses itself in two enormous systems of association, both conscious and unconscious, which profoundly influence the way we picture life and respond to it. With Oneness we associate unity, wholeness, concord, integrity, security; with Multiplicity we associate strife, disorder, enmity, variety, liberty. From Oneness follow stability, composure, endurance, fidelity; from Multiplicity follow anxiety, excitement, impulsiveness, change. Oneness posits the calm certainty of abstract form, Multiplicity the immediacy and imperfection of the material world. Oneness suggests religious love, family love, marital love; Multiplicity suggests the encompassing jeopardous rush of sexuality. Let me arrange these associations more graphically:

---

90. See Francis Bacon, *The New Organon,* I.lv, and Thomas Hobbes, *Leviathan,* Chapter 8. Also John Locke, *An Essay Concerning the Human Understanding,* Book II, especially sections 11 and 25.

THE ONE	THE MANY
love	strife
permanence	change
rest	motion
unity	variety
security	adventure
theory	practice
tameness	wildness
familiarity	strangeness
safety	danger
abstract	concrete
reason	passion
fair dealing	opportunism
tranquility	anxiety
peace	war
certainty	doubt
nature	technology
country	city
prenatal life, infancy	weaning, maturity
conscious	unconscious[91]

These armies of association create two separate domains of cognition/emotion, which may be said to exist in every individual. The Domain of the One carries our dearest associations, our desire for certainty, our need for security, our sense of responsibility and communality, our respect for authority and the desire to assert it. The Domain of the Many connects with our love of pleasure, adventure and discovery, the excitement of the unknown, our

---

91. I make this last distinction because of the ordering devices associated with consciousness and the often chaotic propensities of the unconscious. But as Freud observed, the unconscious has ordering principles of its own — faculties that recast unsettling emotions into dream structures ("dream-works").

sense of individuality, our love of liberty, our fear and insecurity, our anxiety about chaos. The world of the One is our home; the world of the Many is our wilderness. For most of us the interaction of these mental domains is seldom jarring; we walk measured paths between the two worlds, enjoying contrasts, shunning extremes. But profound emotion — love, grief, anger, awe — can force us temporarily into the confines of a single camp. In less balanced character types, one camp will dominate, and behavior will take on recognizable aspects of the mental locale.

Is the One morally superior to the Many? Hardly. The One might accuse the Many of spawning anarchists, criminals and libertines, but the Many would reply by accusing the One of fostering tyrants, cultists and puritans. One and Many are not moral forces; rather, they are premoral cognitive necessities. Morality must be won out of the stress between them.

MODERNITY AS THE DOMAIN OF THE MANY

The associations bred by the One/Many distinction have been documented from early on. Parmenides (the real philosopher this time, not the Platonic character) wrote that the dominant cosmic forces were love (the One) and strife (the Many). Plato set up a full associative array by portraying Socrates (a believer in the One) as an integral, loyal, stable, honest and peace-loving individual, while depicting the Sophists (believers in the Many) as disingenuous, treacherous, inconsistent and tyrannical.[92] But the issue has taken on a special character in modern times. Here is the Renaissance courtier Sir Thomas Wyatt, lamenting lost love:

---

92. On Socrates, see Alcibiades' speech in the *Symposium* (215a–222c); for the Sophists, see the character of Callicles in the *Gorgias* (488b et seq.) or the character of Thrasymachus (*Republic,* Book I).

They flee from me that sometime did me seek
    With naked foot, stalking in my chamber.
I have seen them gentle, tame and meek
    That now are wild, and do not remember
    That sometime they put themselves in danger
To take bread from my hand; and now they range
Busily seeking with a continual change.

Thankèd be fortune it hath been otherwise
    Twenty times better; but once in special
In thin array, after a pleasant guise,
    When her loose gown from her shoulders did fall,
    And she me caught in her armes long and small,
Therewith all sweetly did me kiss,
And softly said, "Dear heart, how like you this?"

It was no dream: I lay broad waking.
    But all is turned, through my gentleness
Into a strange fashion of forsaking;
    And I have leave to go of her goodness,
    And she also to use newfangleness.
But since that I so kindly am served
I would fain know what she hath deserved.

The poem's speaker is an abandoned lover whose values include fidelity, love and stability. The women who have abandoned him are associated with wildness, change and bad faith. But this traditional One/Many distinction is given an unusual twist when, in the third stanza, the poet places special emphasis on "strange fashion" and "newfangleness." These words relate the women's unfaithful behavior to new fashions at court: modes of dress and behavior drawn from the Continent, which were subjects of controversy among Wyatt and his contemporaries. Strangeness and newness are elements of Multiplicity, exciting but full of chaotic potential. Renaissance observers recognized this potential and took sides as to whether innovation was worth the risk.[93]

Of course, the innovations that troubled Wyatt have never stopped. In particular they have crowded into the twentieth century, which has been packed with far more change and surprise than any century before it. The cognitive impact of all this change and surprise is worth noting. To the extent that our social environment has evolved from relative stability to relative change, it has warped from the One to the Many, from the nest of unity to the arena of multiplicity.

This change has played itself out in other dimensions as well. Multiplicity is rampant in the invasive crowdedness of our modern cities, in the frustration of traffic jams and packed supermarkets, in the dehumanizing noises that urban dwellers now accept without complaint. Multiplicity thrives in our crowded calendars, in the flood of information carried to us by mail and over the air, and in the riot of divergent viewpoints so conveyed. As professional specialists trained in narrow disciplines, we view reality from multiplex, often fragmented perspectives, and this sense of fragmentation, an adjunct of the Many, is enhanced by our dependence on indirect modes of communication and the widespread separation of artisans from the products they help to create. Mass-market dynamics separate intellectuals from society at large, thus in effect separating society from itself. Cement, wires, medicines and cheap highs isolate us from nature. The nuclear family has ebbed, percentage-wise, to an all-time low. Crime, class anger

---

93. Supporters of the new included Machiavelli (see Chapter 15 of *The Prince*) and Bacon: "It would be an unsound fancy and self-contradictory to expect that things which have never yet been done can be done except by means which have never yet been tried" (*Novum Organum,* I.vi, trans. James Spedding, reprinted in *Francis Bacon: A Selection of His Works,* ed. Sidney Warhaft [New York: Odyssey, 1965], p. 332). Enemies of the new included Prince Hamlet (Chapter 2 above) and John Donne, whose satirical *Ignatius His Conclave* (1611) depicted Machiavelli and his fellow revolutionaries Copernicus and Paracelsus as denizens of hell.

and ethnic hatreds rage in domestic headlines, while the world is jolted by institutionalized hatred in one global trouble spot after another. Our infants are born in the Domain of the Many, and as children they learn its language and its laws.

ISSUES AS DIALOGIC FORMS

Though packed with countless bizarre temptations, the Domain of the Many is a world of anxiety, frustration and, above all, alienation. It is the birthplace of Sartre's "anguish, forlornness and despair"; it is reminiscent of the unknowable, fallacious and chaotic world envisioned by the Greek Sophists. But one does not have to read philosophy in order to appreciate the particular agony of this domain, or to seek redress for its ills. As I have mentioned in Chapters 7 and 10, various current initiatives, all independently conceived, all classifiable as holistic, are in effect seeking to restore the politics, ethics and psychology of the One.

The idea of wholeness is evocative, compelling and eminently worthy of support. From a political perspective, free society needs all the wholeness it can get, to counteract and complement the effects of the Many. But unqualified wholeness is not a completely satisfying idea, for the simple reason that it does not fully acknowledge the nature of thought. If thought is essentially a dialogic interface of conjunctions (the One) and disjunctions (the Many), then wholeness, as an avatar of the One, speaks to only half the picture. The deep message of Plato's *Parmenides* is that wholeness and fragmentation — the One and the Many — are valuable *only as joint parameters.* They cannot be objects of choice, because they are the nature of choice: they establish the playing field on which choices can be made. As individuals or groups we can warp our course toward one or the other, but attempting a run too near the absolute would rob us of perspective and hence of freedom.

We may conclude something similar regarding other perennial

issues connected with the issue of the One and the Many: issues of individual vs. community, freedom vs. security, nature vs. technology, form vs. content, theory vs. practice, city vs. country, etc. Short-term, practical solutions may emphasize one of the rival parameters over the other, but philosophy will never sort the basic issues out, for the issues lie so close to the roots of thought that thought can have only a limited perspective on them. Because these issues, like the One and the Many, are force fields generated by mutually empowering oppositions, they cannot be tamed, but reassert themselves in ever-new configurations. For this reason, there is something to be said for calling the One and the Many and related issues "dialogic forms," that is, permanent places in the architecture of thought. This nomenclature would be in accord with the implications of the *Parmenides,* which renounces the Socratic theory of forms and replaces it with the dialectical interaction of One and Many. Abstract entities, Plato suggests, have value only as elements in perennial questions; philosophy is most at home in the tension-filled confrontation of opposites.[94]

COPIOUS THINKING AND DIALOGIC FORMS

The inextinguishable vitality of the One/Many distinction and related dialogic forms has proven impervious to Western philosophy. Philosophy as we know it, whether practiced by a Leibnitz or a Spinoza, a Wittgenstein or a Heidegger, is a largely reductive business, an effort to reduce experience and thought to abstract principle. Philosophy as we know it is thus a One-driven project,

---

94. A similar view is stated dramatically by the Platonic philosopher Giordano Bruno in *Degli eroici furori* (1585; translated as *The Heroic Frenzies* by Paul Eugene Memmo), though Bruno goes on to postulate a quasi-divine unity underlying all opposites.

interrupted occasionally by Many-driven counterattacks (the Greek Sophists, the deconstructionists). But our inquiries in this chapter and others suggest that experience and thought do not yield up their secrets to the reductive, the single-minded or the absolute: they demand a more forgiving attitude and a more flexible instrumentation. Copious thinking, as described in Chapter 3, is a methodology of this sort. Embracing rather than confrontational, polymorphic rather than consistent, playful rather than solemn, copious thinking all but imitates the paradoxes and ambiguities of its subject matter. Partaking of both the One and the Many, it is a fitting perspective on a world that is alive with the dialogic stress between them.

Meditations on Dialogue and Sexuality

How do the traditional male and female stereotypes line up in terms of the One and the Many? Confusingly. Women suggest the Many in their easiness with their own emotions, their de-emphasis on power and authority, their changing moods, but they suggest the One as mothers and as symbols of unity with nature. Men suggest the Many in their violence, sexual aggressiveness and love of technology but they suggest the One in their dependence on authority, reason and consistency. Nature, always ready for some fun, has aligned men's chaotic side with women's stable side and vice versa, in the same way that it has aligned their bodies for sexual contact with each other. This dialogic of chaos and stability is a major engine of sexual attraction, intellectual fascination and mutual misunderstanding.

   Like other dialogic forms, gender differentiation can be a source of learning. Talking with members of the opposite sex, observing them, we may learn better ways of responding to situations that have been difficult for us, better ways of treating our own bodies, better work habits, more ways of being amused. The barrier to such learning has been an absurd and retrograde genderal chauvinism.

What essentially can men learn from women, women from men? Conventional wisdom suggests that men can teach women to be more aggressive and less anxious, and that women can teach men to be less aggressive and more caring. But this is superficial and mechanistic: you cannot top up and pour out people like glasses of beer. What women can really teach men is to appreciate what is directly around them, to relax their grip on responsibility and certainty and conclusiveness, to see life as process, to feel and express emotion consciously, to listen to and *listen through* another person's words. What men can teach women is how to develop an architecture of abstract ideas that will then accommodate particular thoughts or instances, how to fall passionately in love with a topic or piece of work, how to coexist peacefully with tools and machines, and how, when possible, to forget everything except the present moment.

∾ "If he doesn't trip and fall, he's got a touchdown!" exclaims a football telecaster while the screen shows a runner who *has* tripped and fallen and is clawing the turf in frustration. The telecaster is indulging in a grammatical innovation of the early 1990s, a means of heightening verbal impact by speaking of a past action as though it were present. In so doing he gives yet another example of the fertile power of athletics, as described on television and radio, to generate linguistic novelty and renew English idiom. He also attests to a fascinating general distinction: that the creation and use of slang has been a predominantly male enterprise. Why is this so? Slang comes from the professions, which have been until recently, and in many cases still are, male-dominated. The necessities of professional life have caused men to use language as a tool for production, discovery and conquest, while women have learned to conceive of language more as a vessel for personal expression. Toolmaker man constantly seeks to sharpen, refine, renew his technology, language included. Woman, who seeks understanding rather than impact, is less in love with novelty.

As the professional ranks swell with women, these distinctions are likely to disappear; women will become wordsmiths like men. This influx of new talent will arouse gyrations of linguistic novelty. But who then will remind the world of its vanity, and who will remember the language of the heart?[95]

❧ Lovemaking is an interpretive loop in which the language is not only words but kisses and caresses and the meaning conveyed is intimacy and affection and pleasure. Lovemaking is thus a dialogue, with each new statement changing both stater and statee, with each excited response becoming a newly exciting statement, all spiraling into a vortex of intensity. What lovemakers create is a four-dimensional work of dialogic art, impermanent yet unforgettable. What lovemakers create is a reciprocal symmetry, corporeal yet formally superior to most philosophy and art.

❧ Sexuality evokes both the One and the Many: the One, because of the utter absorption of the experience, its wholeness; the Many, because of the discovery, the mystery, the strangeness of intimacy. We are drawn, so to speak, by the Many into the One. In marital sexuality this balance is endangered. In marriage, sexuality relaxes into security; husbands and wives walk around the house with no clothes on; spouses stop caring whether or not they are sexually attractive. Marriage thus tends to suppress the Many, deplete the strangeness, leaving husband and wife under the tyranny of the One, in a quasi-sibling relationship interrupted occasionally by some more-of-the-same sex. There are all sorts of practical ways to spiff things up and bring back the excitement, but technique and tactics in themselves cannot permanently revive a

---

95. On males as wordsmiths, see Epstein, *Deceptive Distinctions,* pp. 224–31. Epstein stresses the role of social influences in determining major forms of gender differentiation.

deflated libido. One needs a fundamental change in attitude, even in identity — a change suggested by two questions:

> *Do I acknowledge in my spouse the same inner complexity and potential for passion — the same strangeness and mystery — that I feel in myself?*

And, for more extreme cases,

> *Do I acknowledge these characteristics even in myself?*

I have discussed the ramifications of the first question in Chapter 7 and will look at aspects of the second question in the chapter that follows.

12

⁊⁊⁊

The Stranger in the Mirror:
Patterns of Self-Inquiry

Socrates was once gossiping with some friends about an Athenian who was about to take a voyage. "Will he learn much from his trip?" asked one friend. "Unlikely," replied Socrates. "He's taking himself along." Twenty-four hundred years later, the words still bite deep. Real learning is not, like foraging or money-making, a simple matter of acquisition. It is rather a process in which new experience that one encounters is reciprocated by inner change in oneself. This inner change, this growth, is difficult, if not impossible, if one "takes oneself along," that is, if one confronts every new situation with an armored identity, imposing a familiar perspective on unfamiliar events. This assertive attitude, this obsessive self, is like some government censor blocking any ideas or data that might provoke rebellion. Instead one must be ready to lose the self, or to have a sense of self so flexible and yielding that it poses no threat to the new. This flexible self is not a weak self; it is a stronger, more youthful, more human identity, open to the outrageous variety of experience and the profound surprises of change. Such an identity may be fostered by the regime of self-questioning and self-imaging that I explore in this chapter.

Self-inquiry, that most intimate form of dialogue, is multileveled and many-tongued. It thrives in the complex systems of philosophers and in the simple message of conscience, in the discourse of the communal and the idiom of the individual, in facts we know about ourselves and fictions we conceive in dreams and stories, in the elegant interpretation of the psychoanalyst and in the unexpected moment when, in the twilight, on my way out of the house, I pause and wonder who the stranger in the mirror is. Almost every area in which we think and feel, each in its different way, is charged with the uniquely human faculty of self-reflection.

The variety of valid forms of self-inquiry implies that no *one* form is preeminently effective or universally applicable. Claims notwithstanding, no one system can speak to the full self, no intuition or set of intuitions addresses the whole. It implies as well that the "self" into whom we inquire is likely to be less a discrete and unitary presence than a polymorph: a multiplicity of images and voices, an ever-changing collage of perspectives. The self is telescopic, now stretching to embrace the galaxy, now contracting to the narrow confines of a toothache or stubbed toe. The self is amoebic, capable of almost endless configurations, holding like some repertory company the full cast of human characters and the gamut of emotions. We have manifold reservoirs of identity, and access to one of them often dams up the channels to the others.

In this confusion of perspectives, is effective self-inquiry at all possible? *No,* if I see effective inquiry as systematic progress toward a specific goal. *Yes,* if I adopt a pluralistic perspective, use different methods for different areas of exploration and renounce the goal of some designated product in favor of an ongoing process of discovery.

What reward attends on this practice? Perhaps the most accurate answer is *perspective,* in the broadest sense of the word. Actively self-inquisitive, one can sense one's own multiplicity and capacity for change; one can identify and reduce the forces that produce knee-jerk, self-limiting responses; one can discover and try to heal the conflicts that produce self-defeating behavior patterns. Actively self-inquisitive, one can identify generously with the equally complex nature of another human being and, conversely, hold oneself at arm's length and see oneself with the eyes of a stranger. Self-inquiry does the fullest justice to and is the fullest expression of the dignity of the human being.

Ranked against this are the disadvantages and harms, both to ourselves and to others, of lacking self-perspective. Failure in perspective — distorted understanding of self and of the self's relationship to others — is a nearly universal psychological characteristic of violent criminals. Weak or warped perspective is a sine qua non of nationalism, factionalism, bigotry and cultism; in less extreme forms it is epidemic in society, present equally in the puritan and the libertine, the enthusiast and the dropout, the anxious and the depressed. Without self-reflection there is no ready path to moral equity, and we are led to good or ill by the relatively weak guides of experience, common sense and other people's rules.

THE NATURE OF IDENTITY

Before I ask, "Who am I?" I must establish the ground rules of inquiry by asking, "What can we fairly call the self?" The most helpful answer to this question seems to be the most inclusive. Self is not a naked mind/body divorced from context and isolated in an instant of present consciousness. Self stretches to include our clothing, technologies and habits, everything we identify as our own, everything, corporeal or abstract, that we identify *with,* all on both conscious and unconscious levels. Selfhood extends far beyond us, reciprocating with other people and institutions, even with the nonhuman. Let me briefly sketch, as an example, a fictional identity.

Lester Boyardi is a white male, divorced and childless, age sixty, height five feet nine inches, weight 195 pounds. He commutes by car from his home in Tenafly, New Jersey, to Manhattan, where he is vice president of a large bank. His parents, English and Italian, met in France in the 1920s and emigrated to Idaho, where Lester, the youngest of three brothers, was raised on a ranch near the Sawtooth Mountains. He was educated in a one-room schoolhouse, a distant small-town high school and, after service in the Korean War, the University of Idaho in Boise. He came to New York in the late 1950s, went to accounting school for a few months and then took a job with the bank for which he still works.

Lester is a balding, gentle-eyed, roundish man who considers himself old, overweight and out of shape. His social involvement is limited to his work and a few friends who share his passion for fly-fishing. Chatting and laughing with these men, he is at his ease, most of all when he is regaling them with stories of his Idaho childhood. Weekday evenings, lonely and silent, physically and mentally exhausted, he reads mystery novels or watches television news shows. At work he gets along well with peers and superiors but feels slightly uncomfortable with the younger employees, who on their side think him benign but distant. He is quietly proud of being a bachelor of arts, a banker and a trusted member of a large corporation. He is also proud of being an American but somewhat insecure in the knowledge that his parents were immigrants. His chief professional motives are efficiency, responsibility and the thrill of power, but he is rather cautious and has never aspired to be a CEO. He plans to retire in a few years and build a cabin on some land that he has bought near Bend, Oregon. He wishes to be considered capable and humane. Married early and long divorced, he is acutely shy of women and is not aware of any sexual longings, but he has recurrent dreams of bizarre eroticism. He is furtively addicted to nicotine and caffeine and day-long snacking.

Lester's identity has a variety of modes or levels. He exists as he *thinks himself to be* ("old, overweight and out of shape"), as he *wishes himself to be* (efficient, responsible), as he *wishes to be thought of* ("capable and humane"), as he *is thought of* ("benign but distant") and as he *functions unconsciously* (the addictions, the erotic dreams). He is defined by past geography and culture (rural Idaho), and he defines a future (rural Oregon) that is similar to it. He has two familial identities ("the youngest of three brothers," "divorced and childless"), which perhaps influence his social relationships ("gets along well with peers and superiors but feels slightly uncomfortable with the younger employees"). He defines himself in a specific cultural and economic continuum ("quietly proud of being a bachelor of arts, a banker and a trusted member of a large corporation"). Speaking generally, we may see Lester as partaking of

- conscious identity
- unconscious identity
- willed identity
- familial identity
- identity as perceived by others
- geographic and temporal identity
- generic identities (family, peer group, gender, professional, corporate, class, cultural, linguistic, national).

Our hero is a mélange of identities, a concourse of living vectors that harmonize or conflict, tense up and relax, emerge upon the surface and submerge beneath it.

Lester is an example of the almost limitless complexity that can be found in a perfectly ordinary life. He is not aware of this dramatic complexity. It does not trouble him. Like most mature people, he has unconsciously developed what I call in Chapter 9 a "personal eloquence": a way of harmonizing, or at least compromising with, the forces that define him.

But suppose Lester suffers a deep shock. His eldest brother, Christian, a notable Idaho politician who has always been Lester's hero, commits suicide at a woman's home in Sun Valley; the police begin unfolding a history of kickbacks, sex orgies and underworld ties. Lester is dumbfounded and becomes psychosomatically ill. He visits a psychiatrist, who, after a few mind-opening sessions, recommends that he take his sick leave on a friend's ranch near the Salmon River. This psychiatrist, who is an insightful person, sends Lester back to his roots on a special mission. His goal is not to reconcile himself to Christian's shame and death; only time can do that. His goal is to discover who he really is.

If all this looks like the plot of a novel, the similarity is not coincidental. Many novelists have concerned themselves with self-discovery, with the means by which people recognize and come to terms with their own natures. And the serious novelist — Gustave Flaubert, for example, or Emily Brontë — realizes that an individual's "nature" is not reducible to theoretical shorthand but rather derives from a measureless richness of variables: genes, place, tradition, family, experience, previous choices, etc. In returning to his roots, Lester Boyardi will renew contact, at least in part, with the forces that shaped him as an individual. With senses sharpened by suffering, he will look into faces from the past, he will listen to the language of place, he will fish in the rivers of childhood. If his inquiry is honest and brave, he will regain access to the buoyant energies that impelled his youth.

The form of comprehensive self-inquiry prescribed for Lester goes far beyond the realm of formal disciplines, beyond language itself, into wholly personal, untranslatable messages of feeling. Yet in a philosophical sense, it does not go far enough. The two-paragraph description of Lester is limited to the characteristics that make him an individual. But what of the characteristics that make him human? Can we really know ourselves as individuals without understanding our humanity? Lester's mission of self-healing may fulfill itself happily in Idaho, but our own different quest must take us further, into the studies of humanity: literature, art, philosophy, history, anthropology, psychology. And because general human character is itself individuated from a natural context, we must address the natural sciences as well. Nothing that gives us character is foreign to our inquiry.

An impossibly broad study? Not if one views it as a redefinition of the liberal education that is the staple of our colleges and universities. The "liberal arts" are commonly seen as discrete disciplines that, properly blended, can infuse students with critical thinking, cultural literacy, good taste and communicative skills. These disciplines might be expanded to include technology and commerce. They might then be reintegrated in new ways by a student or teacher who saw them as interconnected media of self-inquiry — as subtle, evocative means of asking "Who am I?"

But if self-inquiry suggests a broadening of the things we study, it also suggests an enrichment of our attitude toward everyday life. I enrich myself by questioning myself about my own goals and habits and occupations, or rather, by giving ear to an inner voice that asks quietly but persistently who I am and what I value. If the questions are earnest and the answers honest, a new image of myself slowly emerges, not of the traditional subjective me but of someone seen from a distance: a human being in a human context.

THE DISCOURSE OF SELF-INQUIRY:
PROFILE, JOURNAL, NARRATIVE

Self-inquiry can be conducted via group therapy, psychoanalysis, psychotherapy, psychological counseling and other clinical or interpersonal means. Here, however, I will confine myself to three forms of personal and informal self-inquiry whose only requirement is the ability to write. The simplest of these, and perhaps the most revealing, would be to write a third-person Lester Boyardi–style profile of oneself in two paragraphs, the first paragraph giving bare vital statistics, the second enlarging on one's own character in terms of both propensities and shortcomings. This may seem a simple enough assignment, but if it is honestly addressed, it can carry with it a surprising amount of excitement and anxiety. These emotions spring from the experience of imprisoning one's own free and expansive character in the confines of a single page, from the stress of admitting the limits of one's aspirations and achievements and from the guilt of owning up to (or consciously suppressing) elements of character that one is embarrassed about.

A second writing exercise, less intrusive but much more extensive, is journal-keeping. In Chapter 4 I discussed the journal as a means by which writers can enhance the dialogue between themselves and the texts they are creating. Journals can serve several other purposes. They can be ways of catching and holding the unique quality of present time. They can commemorate the places we visit, the pursuits we enjoy, the people we love. They can witness secret thoughts. And they can, like sentient mirrors, capture the shapes of our concerns and project them back on us. Serious journal-keeping carries a special kind of power. The mere act of putting intense concerns down on paper throws these concerns into a new dimension and gives us a new perspective on them. The expansion of the journal over weeks, months and years provides a treasury of self-inquiry and a history of characterological continuity and change.

Finally, there is narrative. This might be seen as the most difficult of the three dialogic activities, for narrative is supposed to be an art. But actually bedtime-story skills are all that is needed. Two exercises are of possible value here: the first, to compose a narrative with oneself as protagonist; the second, to split up elements in one's own psyche (e.g., hopes, fears, sense of order, sense of mischief) and make them characters in a story. How do these inventions aid self-inquiry? Psychologists and anthropologists are interested in narration less as conscious imaging than as unconscious self-revelation. Like some chemical reaction releasing latent energies, narrative creativity expresses latent emotions and concerns.

In her book *Invisible Guests,* Mary Watkins enlarges on this esthetic and psychological phenomenon with special reference to what might be called runaway characters: fictional creations who seem to take charge of their authors' minds. Citing Flaubert, Dostoevski, Henry James, Joyce Cary, Flannery O'Connor and Alice Walker, she describes an artistic awareness that "finds" characters rather than creating them, that listens for what they will say rather than putting words into their mouths, and that, rather than forcing them into arbitrary actions, waits for what they must essentially do. Watkins interprets this phenomenon as an "imaginal dialogue," a psychological opening-up and awakening to latent aspects of identity.[96]

Watkins' book is strongly influenced by the work of the psychiatrist Carl Jung, to whom she returns frequently. While Sigmund Freud stressed the role of early personal experience in the development of the unconscious, Jung populated the unconscious with socially determined archetypes, which, endowed with a cer-

---

96. Watkins, *Invisible Guests,* Chapter 7.

tain autonomy, wield significant power over the mind's inner discourse. To Jung these archetypal powers embodied themselves in imaginary (Watkins uses the word "imaginal") figures, to whom he could give names and with whom he could hold dialogues.[97] For Jung these dialogues represented a beneficial unfolding of self, not only in terms of its personal uniqueness but in terms of its social identity.

TOPICS OF SELF-INQUIRY: PAIN AND THE SELF-OTHER INTERFACE

What sort of things do we inquire about in ourselves? A reasonable set of questions, in the spirit in which we approached Lester Boyardi, would be "Who am I? Where am I in life? What do I value? What do I want?" But such an approach may be too general, too benign. Remember that Lester does not inquire into himself until he is shattered by loss. To me there is a strong *confessional* element in real self-inquiry: it includes, perhaps is even predicated on, inquiry into one's private agonies. For the general questions above, we may substitute others: "Am I phobic?" "Am I angry?" "Am I anxious?" "Am I addictive?" We know who we are by knowing how and where we fail. Lester's case suggests that acknowledged pain is the gateway to self-knowledge, and that

---

97. "Jung argues that it is not *we* who personify these figures but they who 'have a personal nature from the beginning' [*Alchemical Studies,* in the *Collected Works of C. G. Jung,* Vol. 13, paragraph 620]. He tries to account for their autonomy with his notion of archetypes. The figures are not considered mere projections but issue from non-personal archetypes, from formative dispositions. The individual characters one experiences are both expressions of one's own ego and also variations on forms which exist independently of the person" (Watkins, p. 19). Also see Jung, *Memories, Dreams, Reflections,* Chapter 6, where he discusses some of his own internal characters.

when hidden wounds are exposed and aired, the identity may reconstitute itself and heal them.

Of course, there are wounds that do not hurt: fears, denials, debilities that are concealed from consciousness. With Lester, these troubles were plastered over by a kind of complacency; they did not surface until prompted by tragedy. Lester's case is epidemic in society. Especially in middle age, the multiple balancing act of work, family and domestic economy may lead to a kind of harried damage-control mentality in which the self loses its shape and is fragmented into a series of intense engagements with tasks. Most people caught in this predicament give little thought to self-inquiry; they are so task-driven that there does not seem to be a self to inquire into in the first place. But for those who do, a method of self-analysis rather different from Lester's may be in order. Using a journal, one may rechart one's identity by examining the interface between Self and Other.

This method is based on three questions that apply to the full gamut of social interactions:

1. *What are the distinctions between my actions as I intend them and my actions as perceived by others?* (E.g., I try to be broad-minded but am criticized for being wishy-washy.)
2. *What moral standards do I apply to my associates (and the world at large), and do I observe these standards in my dealings with others?* (E.g., I expect my associates to trust me with all relevant information, but I have secrets which I must keep from them.)
3. *What sorts of things surprise me?* (E.g., I am surprised when in spite of my generosity, my children show little gratitude and ask more and more of me.)

Asking these questions and answering them with honesty can make me conscious of a new area of identity. Question 1 can bring me into contact with myself *as I am realized by my words and actions.* Question 2 can ease the disparity between my self-consciousness and my awareness of others. Question 3 can expose my fictions about experience and perhaps my reasons for concocting them. Asked as part of an honest self-inquiry, these questions can teach me to see myself, warts and all, as a functioning human being. And from that new perspective I can ask a whole new set of questions.

These forms of self-inquiry can make me aware of a strangeness in myself, as though (as I put it at the start of this chapter) I had looked in the mirror and seen a stranger looking back. And this awareness in turn gives rise to a sense of necessity: that I must accommodate this stranger — strive to change him, perhaps, but in any event acknowledge him as my own. Like my other voices and dimensions, he can be a source of vitality, and perhaps, since he is so involved with my shortcomings, he alone holds the key to renewal.

Self-Inquiry and the One/Many Distinction

The avenue of self-inquiry leads me willy-nilly back to the issue of the One and the Many. Looking for one self, I found many selves, a noisy parliament of voices, a variety of components, some familiar and some strange, some conscious and some unconscious, some controllable and some uncontrollable. This multiplicity suggested inconsistency, anxiety, alienation: a syndrome that I have called the Domain of the Many. Yet in its multifarious energies lay, uniquely, the secret of reintegration. This is possible if the multiple components of identity, so threatening when seen from a monistic perspective, are accepted as voices in a dialogue. This dialogue, this entertainment of multiplex identity, this application of copious thought to self-inquiry, can be cathartic in its power. Its scope of expression can leave the mind cleansed. And when I thus give ear to the Many, the One reemerges, not as an asserted form but rather as a dialogic focus: as the point of convergence of or friction between the various perspectives that I entertain. This focus is self-awareness, self-consciousness. It is in constant change; its only consistency is the honesty of its reports. In this honesty amid change lie the reconciliation of the One and the Many and the integrity of the self.

13

∽∾∽

Conclusion:
The Dialogic Mind

My inquiry up to this point suggests a number of philosophical premises. I will express these as briefly as I can and then ask and try to answer some questions about their implications.

There is no sure distinction between process and product, between the goal and the progress toward it.

Listening is as powerful an act as speaking, reading as writing, asking as answering; and there are no true speakers who are not also listeners, writers who are not also readers, answerers who are not also askers.

Unless they are understood in a context that includes irony, ambiguity and contingency, conclusions are always wrong and assertions always mistaken.

Truth lies in the nameless energies between contraries. The issue is the answer.

Individual identity can never be fully realized unless it is regularly dissolved into dialogue.

Individuals and organizations that interact dialogically with their environments evolve and survive; those that do not are locked in time.

The One and the Many and all of their mutually opposed permutations are inseparable coordinates of one another.

Are these premises liberal or conservative? At first glance they may seem liberal, but in fact they are really quite rigorous, forbidding complacency, outlawing the security of fixed views and systems, imposing on mind and society an athletic regimen of self-questioning. If they are liberal at all, we must redefine liberalism to fit them. Dialogic thinking, like liberalism, thrives on a wealth of perspectives, but unlike liberalism it remains alert to the stress between perspectives — a stress that becomes the focus of its consciousness.

Because it is multi-perspectival, must the dialogic mind dispense with value? No, value is essential to it in a number of ways. First, the dialogic mind studies values as the forces that drive valid individual initiatives. Second, the stress between different values (for example, between liberal and conservative values) is a basic source of dialogic energy. Third, dialogue itself has operative values — inclusiveness, expressiveness, balance, contrast, concentration, complexity. These may seem less moral than esthetic, but they function in service to a sovereign value — *doing justice to reality* — that has moral character. Fourth, dialogic thought, no matter how indefinite and complex it may be, must boil down to the assertion of simple and straightforward values in real-life situations.

Your "premises" have much in common not only with Oriental mysticism (Taoism, Buddhism) but with mysticism in general. Doesn't this make them impractical? On the contrary. As I implied with the parable of the temple, I believe that there are profound ties between the practical and the mystical. The simplest, most basic things in life, the basic operations of life itself, are full of mystical implications. We block out these implications when we diminish experience into monolinear, goal-oriented rationalizations. Dialogic thinking opens our minds to them again.

But doesn't this align you with so-called New Age thinkers who stress the role of the mystical? No, because for them the mystical is more or less a terminus ad quem, while for me it is but one of many equally important and mutually reciprocating perspectives.

Why don't you devote a chapter to dialogic philosophy in the twentieth century? Dialogic thought in this century is an amorphous phenomenon rather than a shared concern. By and large, the prominent dialogic thinkers did not hold dialogues with each other. True, Jung and Buber staged a kind of debate, but this only served to show where they differed. Gadamer refers to Buber briefly, as does Bakhtin, but there was no real dialogue among them.[98] You might say that each of them was following his own distinctive line, with his own authorities and his own disciples.

I don't make this point with much joy. Hyperspecialized intellectual life in this century has kept lots of potentially interactive minds apart. World War II and Soviet repression (Buber emigrated to Jerusalem; Gadamer, albeit unwillingly, complied with the Nazi regime; Bakhtin lived in exile) were alienating factors, too.

How did you become interested in dialogue? My last three books, *Time and the Art of Living, The Grace of Great Things: Creativity and Innovation* and the novel *Book,* all dealt with aspects of human liberty. In *Time and the Art of Living* I tried to show how intimately our freedom is tied up with attitudes toward time; in *The Grace of Great Things* I discussed creativity as a form of liberty. In the novel various ideas from *The Grace of Great Things* were com-

---

98. On the Buber/Jung disagreement, see Friedman, *Martin Buber's Life and Work,* Chapter 7. For Gadamer's and Bakhtin's references to Buber, see Gadamer's *Philosophical Apprenticeships,* pp. 154–55, 171, and Bakhtin's *Dialogic Imagination,* p. 99. Also see Perlina, "Mikhail Bakhtin and Martin Buber."

bined with a new theme — human communication — and developed dialogically as psychodrama. My earliest book, *Mighty Opposites,* discussed dialectical interactions in Shakespeare, and over the years I have been teaching courses on Plato and discussing the process of dialogue. You might say that the writing line and the teaching line converged in this book. But perhaps the strongest influence of all came from my wife, Michaela Paasche Grudin, whose research on dialogic discourse in the work of Geoffrey Chaucer was a fruitful source of ideas.

Have you anything else to say? Because life itself is characterized by open-ended, reciprocal interactions, dialogue and dialogic thought are the closest that human beings can come to imitating life force.

Bibliography

Note: This bibliography omits classic works by Plato, Aquinas and others, which are available in numerous editions.

Aitchison, Jean. *The Articulate Mammal.* London: Unwin-Hyman, 1989.

Arendt, Hannah. *The Human Condition.* Chicago: University of Chicago Press, 1958.

——— . *Thinking.* Vol. 1 of *The Life of the Mind.* New York: Harcourt Brace Jovanovich, 1977.

Bakhtin, Mikhail. *The Dialogic Imagination.* Ed. Michael Holquist. Austin: University of Texas Press, 1981.

Bateson, Gregory. *Mind and Nature.* New York: Dutton, 1979.

——— . *Steps to an Ecology of Mind.* New York: Ballantine, 1972.

Benda, Julien. *The Betrayal of the Intellectuals.* Trans. Richard Aldington. Boston: Beacon Press, 1955.

Bergman, Shmuel Hugo. *Dialogical Philosophy from Kierkegaard to Buber.* Trans. Arnold A. Gerstein. Albany: State University of New York Press, 1991.

Blakeslee, Sandra. "Studies Offer a New Understanding of Myopia." *New York Times,* May 18, 1993, p. B6.

Block, Peter. *Stewardship.* San Francisco: Berrett-Koehler, 1993.

Bloom, Allan. *The Closing of the American Mind.* New York: Simon & Schuster, 1987.

——— . *Giants and Dwarfs.* New York: Simon & Schuster, 1990.

Bruno, Giordano. *The Heroic Frenzies.* Trans. Paul Eugene Memmo. Chapel Hill: University of North Carolina Press, 1964.

Buber, Martin. *Between Man and Man.* Trans. Ronald Gregor Smith. New York: Macmillan, 1965.

————. *I and Thou.* Trans. Walter Kaufmann. New York: Scribner's, 1970.

Carey, John. *The Intellectuals and the Masses: Pride and Prejudice Among the Literary Intelligentsia, 1880–1939.* London: Faber and Faber, 1992.

Cassirer, Ernst. "Galileo's Platonism," in M. F. Ashley Montagu, ed., *Studies and Essays in the History of Science and Learning.* New York: Schuman, 1946, pp. 277–97.

Cave, Terence. *The Cornucopian Text.* Oxford: Clarendon, 1979.

Chamberlin, E. R. *The Bad Popes.* New York: Dial, 1969.

Cmiel, Kenneth. *Democratic Eloquence.* New York: Morrow, 1990.

Cowan, Marianne, ed. *Humanist Without Portfolio: An Anthology of the Writings of Wilhelm von Humboldt.* Detroit: Wayne State University Press, 1963.

Crowther, J. G. *Science in Modern Society.* New York: Schocken, 1968.

Dascal, Marcelo. *Dialogue: An Interdisciplinary Approach.* Amsterdam: John Benjamins, 1985.

Dienstrey, Harris. *Where Mind Meets Body.* New York: HarperCollins, 1991.

Durbin, Paul T. *Dictionary of Concepts in the Philosophy of Science.* New York: Greenwood, 1988.

Emerson, Ralph Waldo. *The Works of Ralph Waldo Emerson.* Vol. 5. Boston: Houghton Mifflin, 1867.

Epstein, Cynthia Fuchs. *Deceptive Distinctions: Sex, Gender and the Social Order.* New Haven: Yale University Press, 1988.

Erasmus, Desiderius. *Adages.* Trans. Margaret Mann Phillips. Toronto: University of Toronto Press, 1982.

————. *On Copia of Words and Ideas.* Trans. Donald B. King and David Rix. Milwaukee: Marquette University Press, 1982.

Evans, R. J. W. *Rudolf II and His World.* Oxford: Clarendon, 1973.

Feyerabend, Paul. *Against Method.* Rev. ed. London: Verso, 1988.

Flader, Susan. *Thinking Like a Mountain: Aldo Leopold and the Evolution of an Ecological Attitude Towards Deer, Wolves and Forests.* Columbia: University of Missouri Press, 1974.

Foucault, Michel. *Les Mots et les choses.* Paris: Gallimard, 1966.

——— . *The Order of Things: An Archeology of the Human Sciences.* Trans. anon. New York: Pantheon, 1971.

Frankfort, Henri, and H. A. Groenwegen Frankfort. *Before Philosophy.* Baltimore: Penguin, 1961.

Frankfurter, Felix. "Alfred North Whitehead," in Alfred North Whitehead, *The Aims of Education.* New York: Mentor, 1949.

Friedman, Maurice. "Introduction," in Martin Buber, *Between Man and Man.* New York: Macmillan, 1965.

——— . *Martin Buber: The Life of Dialogue.* Chicago: University of Chicago Press, 1976.

——— . *Martin Buber's Life and Work: The Later Years, 1945–1965.* New York: Dutton, 1983.

Fukuyama, Francis. *Trust.* New York: Free Press, 1995.

Gadamer, Hans-Georg. *Philosophical Apprenticeships.* Trans. Robert R. Sullivan. Cambridge, Mass.: MIT Press, 1985.

——— . *Truth and Method.* Trans. anon. New York: Crossroad, 1985.

Galvin, Kathleen. *Family Communication.* Glenview, Ill.: Scott, Foresman, 1982.

Gates, Henry Louis, Jr. "Beyond the Culture Wars: Identities in Dialogue," in Modern Language Association, *Profession 93,* pp. 6–11.

Gilbert, Allan, ed. *The Letters of Machiavelli.* Chicago: University of Chicago Press, 1961.

Gleick, James. *Chaos.* New York: Viking Penguin, 1987.

Gould, Stephen Jay. *Eight Little Piggies: Reflections in Natural History.* New York: Norton, 1993.

Grudin, Michaela P. *Chaucer and the Politics of Discourse.* Columbia: University of South Carolina Press, 1996.

Grudin, Robert. *The Grace of Great Things: Creativity and Innovation.* New York: Ticknor & Fields, 1990.

——— . "Humanism," in *Encyclopedia Britannica,* 1986 ed.

——— . *Mighty Opposites: Shakespeare and Renaissance Contrariety.* Berkeley: University of California Press, 1979.

——— . *Time and the Art of Living.* New York: Ticknor & Fields, 1988.

Hausman, Carl R., and Albert Rothenberg, eds. *The Creativity Question.* Durham, N.C.: Duke University Press, 1976.

Heidegger, Martin. *Being and Time.* Trans. John Macquarrie and Edward Robinson. New York: Harper & Row, 1962.

Heinrichs, Jay. "How Harvard Destroyed Rhetoric." *Harvard Magazine* 97, 6 (July–August 1995): 37–42.

Heisenberg, Werner. *Physics and Philosophy.* New York: Harper, 1958.

Heskett, John. "Commerce or Culture: Industralization and Design." *American Center for Design Journal* 6, 1 (1992): 14–33.

Jacobi, Jolande, ed. *Paracelsus: Selected Writings.* Princeton: Princeton University Press, 1958.

James, Henry. *Daisy Miller.* New York: Scribner's, 1937.

Joseph, Lawrence E. *Gaia: The Growth of an Idea.* New York: St. Martin's, 1990.

Jung, C. G. *The Collected Works of C. G. Jung.* Trans. R. F. C. Hull. Princeton: Princeton University Press, 1968.

——— . *Memories, Dreams, Reflections.* Trans. A. Jaffe. New York: Knopf, 1961.

Kauffman, Stuart. *At Home in the Universe.* New York: Oxford University Press, 1995.

Kaufmann, Thomas DaCosta. "The Allegories and Their Meaning," in *The Arcimboldo Effect.* New York: Abbeville, 1987, pp. 89–110.

Kennedy, George A. *Classical Rhetoric.* Chapel Hill: University of North Carolina Press, 1980.

Koestler, Arthur. *The Act of Creation.* London: Arkana, 1989.

————— , and John R. Smythies, eds. *Beyond Reductionism.* New York: Macmillan, 1969.

Kohák, Erazum. *The Embers and the Stars.* Chicago: University of Chicago Press, 1984.

Kuhn, Thomas. *The Structure of Scientific Revolutions.* Rev. ed. Chicago: University of Chicago Press, 1970.

Leeman, Fred, Joost Elfers, and Mick Schuyt. *Hidden Images: Games of Perception, Anamorphic Art, Illusion.* Trans. Ellyn Childs Allison and Margaret L. Kaplan. New York: Abrams, 1976.

Leiss, William. *The Domination of Nature.* Boston: Beacon Press, 1974.

Leopold, Aldo. *A Sand County Almanac.* New York: Ballantine, 1970.

Le Roy, Louis. *Of the Interchangeable Course of Things in the Whole World.* London: C. Yetsweirt, 1594.

Lovelock, James. *The Ages of Gaia.* New York: Bantam, 1990.

————— . *Gaia.* Oxford: Oxford University Press, 1979.

Maranao, Tullio, ed. *The Interpretation of Dialogue.* Chicago: University of Chicago Press, 1990.

Markova, Ivana, and Klaus Foppa. *The Dynamics of Dialogue.* New York: Springer-Verlag, 1991.

Marotti, Arthur. "Love Is Not Love." *English Literary History* 49, 2 (Summer 1982): 396–428.

May, Rollo. *The Courage to Create.* New York: Norton, 1975.

McKeon, Richard. "Dialogue and Controversy in Philosophy," in Tullio Maranhao, ed., *The Interpretation of Dialogue.* Chicago: University of Chicago Press, 1990.

Milosz, Czeslaw. *The Captive Mind.* Trans. Jane Zielonko. New York: Knopf, 1951.

Moyers, Bill. *Healing and the Mind.* New York: Doubleday, 1993.

Murphy, James J., ed. *Renaissance Eloquence.* Berkeley: University of California Press, 1983.

Needham, Joseph. *The Great Titration.* Toronto: University of Toronto Press, 1969.

Nozick, Robert. *The Examined Life.* New York: Simon & Schuster, 1989.

Oppenheimer, J. Robert. *Science and the Common Understanding.* New York: Simon & Schuster, 1966.

Ortega y Gasset, José. *The Dehumanization of Art.* Trans. Helene Weyl. Princeton: Princeton University Press, 1948.

———. *The Revolt of the Masses.* Trans. anon. New York: Norton, 1932.

Parker, Patricia. *Literary Fat Ladies: Rhetoric, Gender, Property.* London: Methuen, 1987.

Perelman, Chaim, and Olbrechts-Tyteca, L. *The New Rhetoric and the Humanities.* Dordrecht, the Netherlands: D. Reidel, 1979.

Perlina, Nina. "Mikhail Bakhtin and Martin Buber: Problems of Dialogic Imagination." *Studies in Twentieth Century Literature* 9, 1 (Fall 1984): 13–28.

Peters, Tom. *Liberation Management.* New York: Knopf, 1992.

Poincaré, H. *The Foundations of Science.* Trans. George Bruce Halsted. New York: Science Press, 1913.

Polanyi, Michael. *Personal Knowledge.* Chicago: University of Chicago Press, 1961.

Prigogine, Ilya, and Isabelle Stengers. *Order Out of Chaos.* New York: Bantam, 1984.

Purver, Margery. *The Royal Society.* Cambridge, Mass.: MIT Press, 1967.

Rabkin, Norman. *Shakespeare and the Common Understanding.* New York: Free Press, 1967.

———. *Shakespeare and the Problem of Meaning.* Chicago: University of Chicago Press, 1981.

Rothenberg, Albert, and Carl R. Hausman, eds. *The Creativity Question.* Durham, N.C.: Duke University Press, 1976.

Rusk, Tom. *The Power of Ethical Persuasion.* New York: Viking Penguin, 1993.

Sacks, Oliver. "To See and Not See." *The New Yorker,* May 10, 1993, pp. 59–73.

Schwartz, Joseph. *The Creative Moment.* New York: HarperCollins, 1992.

Sieburg, Evelyn. *Family Communication.* New York: Gardner, 1985.

Stephens, John. *The Italian Renaissance.* London: Longman, 1990.

Strauss, Leo. *Natural Right and History.* Chicago: University of Chicago Press, 1953.

Tannen, Deborah. *You Just Don't Understand.* New York: Morrow, 1990.

Thomson, Keith. *The Common But Less Frequent Loon.* New Haven: Yale University Press, 1993.

Tjosvold, Dean, and Mary M. Tjosvold. *Leading the Team Organization.* New York: Lexington Books, 1991.

Trinkhaus, Charles. *The Scope of Renaissance Humanism.* Ann Arbor: University of Michigan Press, 1983.

Verderber, Rudolph. *Communicate!* Belmont, Calif.: Wadsworth, 1975.

Waldrop, M. Mitchell. *Complexity.* New York: Touchstone, 1992.

Ward, Peter. *The End of Evolution.* New York: Bantam, 1994.

Watkins, Mary. *Invisible Guests: The Development of Imaginal Dialogues.* Boston: Sigo Press, 1990.

Wellins, Richard S., William C. Byham, and George R. Dixon. *Inside Teams: How 20 World-Class Organizations Are Winning Through Teamwork.* San Francisco: Jossey-Bass, 1994.

Wheatley, Margaret J. *Leadership and the New Science.* San Francisco: Berrett-Koehler, 1992.

Whitehead, Alfred North. *Adventures of Ideas.* New York: Macmillan, 1933.

———. *The Aims of Education.* New York: Macmillan, 1929.

———— . *Process and Reality.* New York: Free Press, 1978.

Wiener, Norbert. *Cybernetics.* 1948. Cambridge, Mass.: MIT Press, 1961.

———— . *The Human Use of Human Beings.* Boston: Houghton Mifflin, 1950.

Wilson, Edward O. *The Diversity of Life.* Cambridge, Mass.: Harvard University Press, 1992.

———— . *On Human Nature.* Cambridge, Mass.: Harvard University Press, 1978.

Wollheim, Richard. *The Thread of Life.* Cambridge, Mass.: Harvard University Press, 1984.

Zajonc, Arthur. *Catching the Light.* New York: Bantam, 1993.

Index of Proper Names